YOU CAN LEAD A BIBLE DISCUSSION GROUP!

"Terry Powell is out to banish boring Bible studies for good. . . .
I enthusiastically recommend this guide to anyone who wants to lead
effective Bible discussions."

Dr. Bruce Wilkinson
Walk Thru The Bible Ministries

YOU CAN LEAD

A BIBLE DISCUSSION GROUP

DR. TERRY POWELL

◈

MULTNOMAH BOOKS
SISTERS, OREGON

YOU CAN LEAD A BIBLE DISCUSSION GROUP
published by Multnomah Books
a part of the Questar publishing family

© 1996 by Terry Powell

International Standard Book Number: 0-88070-884-0

Cover design by Kevin Keller

Printed in the United States of America

Most Scripture quotations are from:
New American Standard Bible
© 1960, 1977 by the Lockman Foundation
Also quoted:
The Holy Bible, New International Version (NIV)
© 1973, 1984 by International Bible Society,
used by permission of Zondervan Publishing House
The Living Bible (TLB)
© 1971 by Tyndale House Publishers

96 97 98 99 00 01 02 03 — 10 9 8 7 6 5 4 3 2 1

To ROBERTSON MCQUILKIN

Missionary, college president, and husband extraordinaire.
If others ever respect me half as much as I respect you,
I'll be a whopping success.

Members of the Team

WRITING THIS BOOK was a team effort. Members of the team include Dolly, my bride of twenty-five years. Her loyal love, calm demeanor, and unwavering faith create a home environment second to none. Then there's Cindy Reeves. Without her computer expertise, copyreading skills, and tireless efforts, the book's content would still be confined to a handwritten draft on a legal pad.

Team members who read the manuscript and offered concrete suggestions for improvement include Rick Perrin, Tim Hanley, Mary Faith Phillips, plus Jeff and Kathy Williams. I can't count high enough to put a price tag on their objective perspectives and encouragement.

And how can I forget the godly leaders who originally motivated and equipped me for a Bible teaching ministry? One class with the enthusiastic Lois LeBar drew me to the field of Christian education like iron shavings to a magnet. Larry Richards taught me how to *think* about the teaching-learning process. More than once, Warren Benson changed my life by modeling the interpersonal dimension of teaching. May our Lord permit me to serve as someone else's Lois, Larry, and Warren.

Contents

Getting Acquainted with the Book's Personality

The pages that follow are chock-full of illustrations, teaching principles, discussion-leading strategies, and sample discussion questions. My intent is to *show* you, within the text, how to prepare and present effective Bible lessons. To *show* you, rather than *tell* you how to lead discussions, requires me to describe scores of interaction techniques and provide numerous checklists.

Why am I explaining the nature of the book up front? Because I don't want you to get lost in the maze of detail I've inserted in some of the chapters. My writing style is informal and conversational rather than academic. You'll encounter humor on a few pages. The flow of thought is smooth rather than disjointed. Yet *You Can Lead a Bible Discussion Group* is essentially a *handbook*, a term emphasizing its long-term usefulness as a reference. Read it now to orient you to the intricacies of discussion leading. But in the future, consult specific chapters or specialized segments on an "as needed" basis.

This book will help you if you use it, rather than just *read* it!

A PERSONAL WORD

LETTERS ARE a "first-class" way to communicate. If I say anything in this book that you want to salute, to shoot down, or to discuss at greater length, drop me a note. When it comes to leading Bible studies or training those who do, we're all in this together.

Let me know if I can personally assist your church, denomination, mission enterprise, or school in the training of Bible teachers. I'm available for on-site consultation or conferences. Seminar subjects include, but aren't limited to, the topics in this book.

Terry Powell
Columbia International University
Post Office Box 3122
Columbia, SC 29230
Phone: 803-754-4100
Fax: 803-786-4209

CHAPTER ONE

The Challenge and Value of Bible Discussions

EVERY SUNDAY EVENING, five couples meet in Jim's den. He has been the designated Bible study leader a grand total of six weeks, guiding discussions on the book of Ephesians. He's happy with how things are going.

Except for Barbara's participation. "You can tell she studies the passage ahead of time," Jim explains. "And she's excited about what she's learning. But she's *too* quick to answer my questions. It's getting to the point where others are slipping into a passive mode. You know, they're just waiting for her to reply. *How can I get others involved in the discussion without stifling Barbara's enthusiasm?*"

❋   ❋   ❋

The Smiths miss the fellowship and top-notch Bible teaching they left behind when they moved. In their new location, they visited First Church and decided to try out a small group. But they left the session frustrated instead of fulfilled.

The folks were friendly enough. What bothered the Smiths was the discussion leader's handling of Scripture. "It was as if human opinion, instead of the Bible, was the authority," commented Steve. "A lot of his questions amounted to 'What does this passage mean to you?' I can't recall probing for what the verses *said*. And some of the unchallenged replies he received seemed off the wall."

❋   ❋   ❋

1

Dennis and Fran took over the senior high Sunday school class a month back. It's their first crack at teaching teens, their only previous experience being in the Primary department. They work hard preparing the Bible lessons. But when they try to get the kids involved in discussion, they're met with a lot of blank stares and shrugs.

"It could be the kind of questions we're asking," remarks Fran, "since we're new at teaching people who can reason through a text. But there's more to it than that. Something is missing. It's like we don't have any rapport with them."

"Last week the atmosphere of the group was several degrees below freezing," adds Dennis. "Wish there was some way to heat things up, to increase their excitement about learning."

✳   ✳   ✳

On Thursdays, Vickie leads a ladies' Bible study at the church. Getting them talking isn't a problem, and the ladies are eager to learn the Bible! But Vickie's a little uncomfortable with the amount of time they spend on doctrinal discussions.

"Seems like we seldom get around to application," Vickie laments, "and when we do, we speak in generalities rather than citing concrete ideas. And as the leader, I accept the responsibility for it. God has given me a knack for spotting principles in the texts, and for posing analytical questions. But dealing with the *So what?* of truth is something else again. I don't really think in terms of practical implications. *What can I do to teach for transformation instead of just information?*"

✳   ✳   ✳

A well-intentioned monopolizer. A group leader who unwittingly discourages in-depth study with the wording of his questions. A couple who shivers in response to the climate in their youth class. A respected ladies' teacher who feels inadequate to explore Bible application. Can you identify with any of these challenging situations?

If so, this book is for you—someone who teaches the Bible, and especially if you use discussion to stimulate learners' thinking.

You won't find sterile theory between these covers. Nor out-of-date prescriptions for group illnesses. You *will* find plenty of ideas forged in the furnace of twenty-five years of teaching. Practical, hands-on ideas. Group interaction strategies you can use this week. Preparation tips that will catapult you toward top-notch discussion leadership.

And I won't just *tell* you how to improve. I'll *show* you. Whenever I cite a teaching principle or offer a guideline for Bible study questions, you can expect concrete examples to follow, caboose-style. After all, we both want a book that *forms* you, not just informs you. With a little help, you *can* lead productive Bible study discussions!

In the remainder of this opening chapter, I'll explore a serious fallacy related to leading discussions. I'll also pinpoint components of an effective Bible discussion, preview the topics addressed throughout the book, and examine eight advantages of discussion-oriented Bible studies.

Taking Discussion for Granted

We had been meeting over breakfast once a week to go over Randy's plans for his Sunday school class. He was leading a singles' group through the book of James. We'd go over his notes on the passage and talk about how to lead the group. Gradually, Randy was warming up to the idea of using other methods to supplement his preferred style: lecture.

I thought Randy was making progress—until the week he showed up without having prepared. "Don't worry," he told me. "This week is a breather. I've decided just to lead a discussion of the passage."

Randy had swallowed a myth about teaching that's as old as Methuselah: *Leading a Bible discussion is a whole lot easier than lecturing. The more I plan to involve learners, the less time it takes to prepare.*

This "discussion is easier" viewpoint deserves a quick burial. And I'm not alone in my bone-deep belief that teachers treat discussion too casually. In a textbook for college teachers, Maryellen Weimer says:

> As an instructional practice, questioning may be the most common, widely used, and universally accepted instruction strategy. *And therein lies the problem. It is too much taken for granted and too much used without insight or conscious awareness.* . . . Questions can make students think and

they can stimulate interest . . . but some ways of using questions are more effective than others. . . . *Clear, cogent, well-sequenced questions are not prepared on the spot. Discussion is an activity for which we must prepare.*[1]

Yes, you can lead compelling discussions of God's Word. But not if you think guiding a discussion is easy. Not if you take the interaction process for granted by skimping on preparation. Not if you shoot from the hip when you ask Bible study questions. Not if you neglect the advice in this book.

Swallow the "discussion is a snap" myth and your Bible study group will soon need resuscitation. But heed the tips in the chapters that follow, and you'll close the lid once and for all on a discussion-killing misconception about teaching.

In this book, you'll discover what Randy learned the hard way. *Bible discussions are a challenge, not a snap!* But you'll also discover ways to lead thought-provoking, effective Bible studies.

DEFINING DISCUSSION

If you crack open a dictionary and locate the verb "discuss," you'll find that it comes from a Latin word that means "to shake apart." We use the word "discuss" to describe verbal interaction generated by mental activity. When two or more folks discuss an issue or a concept, they bounce it around in their minds and examine it. They take it apart, or "shake it apart," and examine it a piece at a time—to enhance understanding or arrive at a conclusion. So a "discussion" is the process of talking about something in an attempt to understand it or arrive at some conclusion.

Discussion, as applied to Bible teaching, is a cooperative search for God's timeless truth and the bearing it has on our lives. All Bible discussion should be done in prayerful reliance on the Holy Spirit to illuminate God's Word and to guide the interaction. Beyond this, successful Bible discussions have at least six components:

- *A teacher or facilitator who originates and directs the conversation*
- *One or more questions to incite thought*
- *A meaningful, specific goal for verbal interaction*
- *Two or more interested participants*

- *An authoritative source of truth (God's Word)*
- *A supportive learning environment*

Take the following definition to heart. By the time you finish this book, you'll know why I crafted it in this precise manner.

Effective Bible discussion, generated by a hospitable learning environment, is a guided conversation that involves people in observing, interpreting, and applying God's Word.

This definition pertains to a variety of learning contexts. Do you teach teens or adults? Do you huddle around your fireplace with a small, fellowship-oriented group, or line up in rows of chairs in a church classroom? Is your forum an evangelistic Bible study at your office during lunch break, or a heavy-duty study with mature Christians?

Your setting may be a church facility, a house, an office, or a classroom. Your learning environment may be tightly regulated or informal. You may advocate discovery learning or prefer a more teacher-centered approach. But whatever your setting or style, if you pop a question now and then, you *are* a discussion leader. And you'll be interested in the practical pointers on the following pages.

TRACKING TOPICS

The next couple of pages preview the topics I cover. I'll whet your appetite with questions that the book chapters address.

? In what type of learning environment do lively discussions thrive? How can I generate a favorable climate for Bible learning? What strategies will accelerate assimilation of visitors? (Chapter 2)

? Which is more important: the preparation phase of a Bible study, or its presentation? Why? (Chapter 3)

? When I start studying a Bible passage, what kind of things do I look for? Are some facts more important than others? How can I turn my choicest observations into questions? (Chapter 3)

? How can I guide learners to discover and to articulate timeless Bible truths? How do I involve them without their reading into the text something God never intended? What distinguishes sound interpretation questions from inferior ones? (Chapter 4)

? What are the distinguishing characteristics of teaching that changes lives? What type of questions steers learners' thoughts to a truth's implications for life? (Chapter 5)

? How can I organize my notes and study questions to fit into the allotted time for the Bible lesson? Can you suggest a logical, step-by-step format for structuring the group session? (Chapter 6)

? What does a full-fledged Bible discussion look like on paper? Can you give me examples of from-start-to-finish lesson plans that rely heavily on questions? (Chapter 6)

? How important are the actual words I use to construct a question? What common mistakes do leaders make in their wording of questions? (Chapter 7)

? After I've posed a question, what are some procedural guidelines to insure qualitative interaction? When a group member answers, what teacher behaviors prompt others to enter the discussion? What leader behaviors stifle further involvement? (Chapter 8)

? When a group member goes off on a tangent or monopolizes the discussion, how should I react? Can I prevent these problems from surfacing in the first place? What keeps a group conversation from degenerating into a "pooling of ignorance"? How should I approach controversial doctrines that tend to drive a wedge between folks of different church backgrounds? (Chapter 9)

? How can local churches and schools train better leaders of Bible discussions? What particular procedures and educational strategies can increase the competency of Sunday school teachers and small group leaders? (Appendices A and B)

? What pertinent findings can discussion leaders glean from social science research? For instance, what have investigators discovered about the role of humor in instructional settings? The influence of a teacher's self-disclosure? The effect of teacher enthusiasm? The impact of a leader's nonverbal communication? The correlation between a question's length and its clarity? The effects of a teacher's reaction to learner contributions? (Scattered throughout the book)

Now that you've had a peek at coming attractions, zoom your mental lens in on the benefits of Bible discussions.

DETERMINING DIVIDENDS

Even if you're already sold on discussion and serve as a facilitator in your group instead of an instructor, you can probably increase the effectivess of your teaching by using good questions. Here are eight ways that discussion profits both learners and leaders:

1. Multiplies Motivation—Teachers who weave questions into the fabric of their studies provide incentive for learning. The opportunity to participate in the learning process enhances students' motivation. Teens and adults who investigate and report on Scripture feel valued. One high school senior was happy to conclude, "What I think matters." Students of all ages appreciate hearing what others think.

According to the authors of *The Act of Teaching*, discussion meets several inherent needs of learners:

- The need to seek diversion and change
- The need to give others information
- The need to attract a certain amount of attention to oneself
- The need to receive feedback in the form of praise and commendation
- The need to form associations and friendships[2]

Perhaps you aren't comfortable meeting some of these needs in Bible study settings. That's okay. But don't ignore the pluses of varying your methods and giving learners a moment in the spotlight.

2. Facilitates Feedback—Show me a group or class where verbal interaction thrives, and I'll show you a leader who's receiving helpful information from and about his learners. *Discussion methods allow teachers to become students of their learners!*

When participants answer questions or pose their own, you find out how well they're grasping concepts. You determine whether they're digesting the material, or whether you should proceed at a slower pace. You discover the level of their Bible study skills. And you detect attitudes or emotional baggage that can affect their receptivity to God's Word.

When instructors aren't interested in feedback, learners know it. A teacher appears insensitive to people's needs when he relies excessively on lecture. "When teachers lecture the whole time," reported a college student, "it shows they aren't concerned about how I'm understanding the material."[3]

3. Fosters Fellowship—Discussion not only acquaints the leader with group members, but also improves group members' relationships with each other. In response to questions, people's beliefs, attitudes, and personal experiences surface. Participants identify with each other's comments and sympathize with personal needs. Whether verbal exchanges occur on an intellectual or an emotional level, discussion requires self-revelation. And self-revelation is a catalyst for creating community.

4. Elicits Encouragement—Rick and Barb led eight couples through a "Parenting from Proverbs" course. During a session on disciplining children, Ken constantly furrowed his brow and fidgeted in his seat. Clearly, something was bothering him.

When Rick asked for examples of how to correct a child, Ken vented his emotions. That very day he had jumped to conclusions and spanked his seven-year-old son. Later, Ken discovered that a sibling had committed the offense. Ken told the group how broken he felt when he discovered his error. He had wept, asked his son to forgive him, and knelt by the boy's bed to seek the Lord's forgiveness.

"The incident demoralized me," admitted Ken. "I'm still feeling bad about it. I wonder if I bruised my son's spirit or drove a permanent wedge between us. You know, you hear about how kids remember something like that the rest of their lives."

After a half-minute of silence, Randy, an older man with three children, responded: "Ken, I commend you for serving as a *positive* model to your son. I don't think he'll remember the unjust spanking. But he'll *never* forget his dad's tearful apology. And the sight of you kneeling by his bed, seeking God's forgiveness, is burned into his memory forever. You modeled how to handle sin. I'd be worried only if you had been too proud to admit you blew it."

That fresh perspective buoyed Ken's spirit and enabled him to forgive himself. Randy's remarks reminded Ken that God wants moms and dads to model Christian living, not perfection.

As the parenting course progressed, other encouraging episodes transpired. One week Rick and Barb scrapped half their discussion questions so the group could pray for one couple's troubled adolescent. The Williamses told how they received valuable tips from a paperback that the Jordans had recommended in the opening session. After a session on "listening skills," group members used the telephone to hold each other accountable for application strategies they had formulated.

The parenting course offered four examples of encouragement spawned by a discussion approach to Bible study: A fresh, biblical perspective promoted a dad's emotional healing; intercessory prayers sustained a hurting mother and father; a recommended resource brought focus to one couple's fuzzy thinking; and telephone inquiries furnished incentive for lesson follow-through. Ask good questions, and you enhance mutual concern and encouragement.

5. Increases Insight—Discussion participants learn from one another, not just from the designated leader. It's the two-heads-are-better-than-one principle applied to exploring God's Word.

Picture a teacher-centered context where the leader holds impressive credentials and prepares extensively. Even in this setting, when the teacher poses a question, somebody much lower on the knowledge totem pole may offer a valid, fresh insight on the Bible text. And the teacher may even learn something! *Effective discussions allow teachers to become learners, and learners to become teachers.*

In their book *Pilgrims in Progress,* Jim and Carol Plueddemann identify three sources of knowledge in a group of Christians: (1) God's Word; (2) the personal experiences of participants; and (3) the insights into the passage contributed by members. They recognize the fallibility of human interpretations and acknowledge that people's experiences must be filtered through the objective authority of Scripture. Yet they believe a successful leader employs all three kinds of knowledge—not separately, but blended together. "Good methods for small groups," they write, "use all the resources of the Holy Spirit—relating the experiences of life with the authority of Scripture in interaction with other Christians."[4]

Allow me a qualifying remark. The extent of this benefit depends on the maturity level or spiritual background of group members. In general, the longer people have known Christ—the longer they've been under the influence of solid Bible teaching—the more valuable their contributions during a Bible study. You can use discussion successfully even with the unchurched in an evangelistic study. But what any participant gleans from the text will be in direct proportion to the illumination provided by the Holy Spirit. That's why the quality of discoveries escalates in a group of maturing believers.

6. Raises Retention— The right questions serve as a mental crowbar, prying open the Bible passage for participants. Group members stitch together noteworthy facts, arrive at timeless conclusions, then articulate the truths they discover. This process requires cerebral activity that tucks the content deeper into their minds.

In experiments measuring the retention of college course information, the transfer of knowledge to new situations, and the extent of problem-solving and attitude change, "the results show differences favoring discussion methods over lecture."[5] One study found little difference between lecture and discussion on measures of *immediate* recall, but a significant superiority for discussion on a measure of *delayed* recall.[6]

Imagine that you've just seen or heard some vital information. To rephrase that information in your own words demands thinking. Researchers suggest that you'll more readily remember the thought you formulated than the information that prompted it.

Bill McNabb and Steven Mabry offer an example of this principle. In *Teaching the Bible Creatively,* they cite an investigation at the University of Toronto:

> People can more easily recall information they have produced than information they have been told to memorize. Subjects who were given the word *rapid* and who were asked to produce a synonym beginning with the letter *f* later remembered the word *fast* better than people asked directly to remember *fast.*[7]

To *tell* the truth is a lofty calling. And so is discussion leadership that guides folks to God's truth, then helps them remember it.

7. Strengthens Study Skills — Individuals who stick with a discussion-oriented group for at least a few months begin to polish their Bible study skills. Week after week they hear questions that point them to God's Word for answers. *Gradually they learn how to think about a Scripture passage.*

Imagine you're leading a group through Ephesians. You start each session with a few probes that help people discover important facts in the text. Only then do you ask them to analyze the data for meaning. Without devoting a session to Bible study methods, you're helping people learn to base interpretations on facts. If you reserve time each week to discuss the practical implications of truths you uncover, you'll increase the likelihood that people will mull over applications when they read the Bible on their own.

Teaching is one thing. Teaching people how to learn is another. *A stimulating Bible discussion educates by its process as well as by its content.*

8. Locates Leaders—Discussion groups provide fertile soil for the development of new teachers and facilitators. How can you spot budding leaders? Mull over the following questions and see who comes to mind.

- *Who demonstrates commitment to the group through regular attendance and consistent completion of assignments?*
- *Who participates regularly without monopolizing the conversation?*
- *Who shows sensitivity to other participants by complimenting their insights or probing for their views on a subject?*
- *Whose answers to study questions reveal keen analysis and concern for sound Bible interpretation?*
- *Who exhibits an infectious enthusiasm for God's Word?*
- *In response to questions, who articulates in a clear, compelling manner?*

Did someone's picture emerge within the frame provided by those questions? If so, inform him of his leadership potential. Encourage her to volunteer for a Sunday school class or lead a small group of her own. Better yet, serve as a trainer by inviting this person to work with you in planning and presenting Bible discussions. Ease the person into a leadership role gradually by increasing responsibility and offering supportive feedback.

❋   ❋   ❋

I applaud you for starting this book. You have demonstrated a craving for excellence. It shows you're interested in the people in your group, not just the content you're covering. In learning, not just teaching.

Since you're hungry for help as a discussion leader, let's press on to Chapter 2. You'll identify the kind of learning environment that spawns successful interaction.

CHAPTER TWO

CREATING A CLIMATE FOR DISCUSSION

A LOCAL ADVERTISING periodical offered the following disclaimer: "Just in case you find mistakes in this paper, please remember they were put there for a purpose. Some folks are always looking for mistakes, and we try to please everyone!"

Now that's an original way to cover your tracks! Just make light of any failures somebody might spot. Then no one thinks twice about them.

When it comes to making mistakes we're all pros, but a few folks have mastered the art of blowing it. You'll find plenty of examples in Stephen Pile's *The Book of Failures:*

- In 1962, a Decca record company executive refused to give an upstart British rock group a contract. "We don't like the Beatles' sound," he explained. "Groups with guitars are on their way out."
- Simon Newcomb (1835-1909) quipped, "Flight by machines heavier than air is impractical and insignificant . . . utterly impossible."
- In 1837, music critic Philip Hale blurted, "If Beethoven's Seventh Symphony is not by some means abridged, it will soon fall into disuse."
- Between 1962 and 1977, Arthur Pedrick patented 162 inventions. That sounds impressive, but none of them ever earned him a penny. That's because his imagination was too far removed from reality. For instance, he planned to irrigate the world's deserts by sending a constant supply of snowballs from the polar region through a massive network of giant peashooters.

13

- During the firefighters' strike in England in 1978, the British Army took over emergency firefighting. On January 14, an elderly lady in South London asked the soldiers to retrieve her cat from a tree. Afterward, the grateful owner invited the troop of heroes in for tea. A few minutes later, waving good-bye, the soldiers backed the fire truck over the cat and killed it.
- "You'll never amount to very much" — the words of a Munich schoolmaster to ten-year-old Albert Einstein.[1]

A head-in-the-clouds inventor who couldn't keep his feet on the ground. A record company executive and music critic who later choked on their own words. British soldiers who celebrated their heroism a bit too soon. A school teacher who misjudged a student. These mistakes stand head and shoulders above run-of-the-mill slip-ups.

However, when it comes to leading a discussion, these blunders pale in comparison to the mistake of taking the group's learning environment for granted. We flirt with failure when we're insensitive to the factors that either stimulate or stifle learners' participation.

This chapter is based on the principle that *effective Bible discussion depends on the learning atmosphere, or "feeling tone," of the group.* Is the social climate warm? Discussion flourishes. Are atmospheric conditions icy or threatening? Discussion fizzles. If you disregard critical factors that affect the learning atmosphere, you'll become a prime prospect for fame — as an entry in *The Book of Failures, Volume II.*

Do a few of your group members seem frozen in their seats? It isn't too late to thaw them out. In this chapter you'll find seven strategies for creating a warmer climate that fosters discussion. As you read, consider the temperature of your group in relation to each factor.

CARING

Charles Swindoll tells of an ex-marine who compared the atmosphere in his church to that of a tavern.

> I have an old Marine buddy who became a Christian several years after he
> was discharged from the Corps. When news of his conversion reached me,

I was pleasantly surprised. He was one of those guys you'd never picture as being interested in spiritual things. He cursed loudly, drank heavily, fought hard, chased women, loved weapons, and hated chapel service. He was a great Marine. But God? They weren't on speaking terms when I bumped around with him.

Then one day we ran into each other. As the conversation turned to his salvation, he frowned, put his hand on my shoulder, and admitted: "Chuck, the only thing I miss is that old fellowship all the guys in our outfit used to have down at the slop shoot (Greek for tavern on base). Man, we'd sit around, laugh, tell stories, drink a few beers, and really let our hair down. It was great! I really haven't found anything to take the place of that great time we used to enjoy. I ain't got nobody to admit my faults to . . . to have 'em put their arms around me and tell me I'm still okay."[2]

Swindoll's friend voiced the deep-felt need everyone has for acceptance and love. *The first critical factor in establishing a positive learning climate is the development of a caring environment.* Your group or class — *not a bar* — is an ideal setting for meeting people's need for acceptance. When leaders show genuine interest in people and when members of a group put a premium on relationships, Bible discussions receive a boost. Participants are more apt to answer and to ask questions when they know others in the room care about them.

The interpersonal dimension of a Bible teaching ministry was paramount to the apostle Paul. While reminiscing about his ministry among the Thessalonians, he wrote, "Having thus a fond affection for you, we were well-pleased to impart to you not only the gospel of God but also our own lives, because you had become very dear to us" (1 Thessalonians 2:8).

Consider these three tips for creating a caring environment:

- *Learn the names of group members and call people by their names regularly.* For large classes, take Polaroid pictures of all participants. Ask everyone to write his or her name just below the image. After you've flipped through the photos a few times, linking names with faces will be a cinch. To help group members learn each other's names, display the photos on a bulletin board.

- *Write encouraging notes to group members.* Salute someone who exhibits enthusiasm for learning. Express gratitude to a person who comforted a hurting group member. Encourage participants who have teaching potential. Follow up on a prayer request voiced during a session.

Consider designing your own postcard and having it printed by a local printer. For a few dollars, you'll get hundreds of personalized cards that will expand your ministry of encouragement. Be sure to write the notes yourself. A handwritten paragraph adds a personal touch unmatched by a keyboard or typewriter.

- *When a class or group meets for the first time, use a "get-acquainted" activity or two.* Don't delve into content right off the bat. Note the following examples:

Designer Name Tags—When our group of twelve met for the first time, the leader distributed blank name tags. Then he asked us to write or print our names in the shape of something that describes us: a personal attribute, current circumstance, interest, or hobby.

To spur our thinking, he provided two examples. Someone who enjoys pickup basketball games could print the letters of his name to form a circle. A group member considering a career change or facing unanswered questions about her future could arrange the letters in the shape of a question mark.

When we finished our "designer name tags," everyone explained his or her creation. Then others asked about the personal experience or sphere of interest captured in the design. Soon the room was humming with conversation. Before we knew it, we felt like old friends, not casual acquaintances.

-ING Words — Ask everyone to think of three -ING words that disclose personal information. (A chef might think of "cooking." An insurance agent might opt for "selling." A new member of Weight Watchers might choose "dieting.") Have every member of a small group share these words with the others. If you teach a large Sunday school class, turn it into a mixer. Tell everyone to meet three folks they don't know well, then use the -ING words as a mode of introduction.

Pleasant Experiences — Give each participant a 3-by-5 card. Have each person describe on the card a pleasant experience from recent months. Instruct people to avoid revealing their identity through anything they write on the cards. Collect the cards, scramble them, and have every participant pick a card. When everyone has received a card other than his own, instruct people to find the person whose experience is recorded on the card.

LAUGHTER

Humor surfaces naturally when folks enjoy being together. Don't feel constrained to collect an arsenal of jokes and fire a volley at the group each week. It *is* wise, however, to plant a humorous anecdote in a lesson when you can connect it to a concept or principle from the Bible passage.

I once taught a sobering lesson on the evidence of moral erosion in King Solomon's life. The older he got, the more foolishly he acted. To introduce this high-profile exception to the "older is wiser" rule, I offered a few telltale signs of aging:

You know you're growing old when . . .

- your "little black book" contains only names ending in M.D.
- your back goes out more than you do.
- you lean over to pick up something off the floor, and you start wondering, *now what else can I do while I'm down here?*
- you sit in a rocking chair and can't make it go.
- you step out of the shower and you're glad the mirror is all fogged up!

The group thoroughly enjoyed the humor, and I linked it into the theme of the character study.

Researchers have discovered a principle about humor in the college classroom that has implications for church teachers and small group leaders. Laughter that isn't associated with ridicule, satire, or other forms of sharp "put down" humor is a social lubricant for the learning environment. The absence of appropriate humor in small group interaction settings may be an indicator of poor bonding.[3]

The value of humor isn't restricted to the social dimension. One researcher found that student satisfaction with learning improves because laughter following humor has a liberating effect on the flow of ideas.[4] Others have identified a correlation between recall of course content and the use of instructional humor.

Researchers found no difference between "straight" and humorously presented information retention immediately after a lecture. However, upon retesting six weeks later, "a statistically-significant, positive effect on content retention was found for students present in the humorous lessons . . . The planned use of humor can spark student recall long after the lesson is over."[5]

How does humor enhance recall of information? Comedy writer Gene Perret may have the answer:

> Comedy is largely graphic. A funny image appears in the mind of the lis-
> tener or learner. We may paint this picture with words, but the real joke is
> in the image that each person sees . . . Since images are more easily
> remembered than are abstract ideas, and since humor is largely visual, it
> stands to reason that using comedy in an illustration will help people
> remember the ideas you are conveying longer and better.[6]

Looking for resources guaranteed to generate chuckles? Go to the humor section of a book retailer and look for Richard Lederer's *Anguished English* and *More Anguished English*.[7] You'll enjoy the examples of botched communication by everybody from courtroom lawyers to church secretaries. Or get a copy of Ross and Kathryn Petras' *The 776 Stupidest Things Ever Said*.[8] Add to your shopping list a series of paperbacks by Jay Leno, containing true but ridiculous headlines he has collected over the years.[9] Quotes from sources such as these evoke laughter and pave the way for positive interaction with God's Word.

INTERCESSION

Missionary spokesman David Bryant calls prayer "rebellion against the status quo." To pray for your group members, and to reserve meeting time for them to pray for one another, acknowledges dependence on the Holy Spirit. And it shuttles them from the "spiritual status quo" to greater Christlikeness. Folks who bear each other's burdens in this manner will feel free to ask or respond to questions during a Bible study. Take a cue from Paul's prayers in Ephesians 3:14–19 and Philippians 1:3–5. On every page of his Day-Timer you'd find time set aside for intercession.

Mull over the following ways to enhance the ministry of intercession within your group.

- *Tag the following questions on to the end of your Bible studies.* What personal needs has the Holy Spirit exposed during this study? How can we pray with you about those needs?

- *Link times of intercession to lesson application.* In a study I led on "The Ministry of Encouragement," everyone shared with a partner the names of people who were experiencing discouraging circumstances. After listing concrete, realistic ways to encourage those in need, everyone prayed for his partner to follow through on at least one idea. If you have a close-knit group, ask everyone to huddle with one or two others before dispersing. They can brainstorm for application ideas and pray for each other's follow-through.

- *Lead a Bible study on the theme of intercessory prayer.* Examine the biblical basis for this expression of group life and discuss ways to exercise intercession in relation to one another. For instance, my title for Nehemiah 1 is "The Ministry of Intercession." The following questions directed learners into the passage and encouraged application:

    What need prompted Nehemiah's intercession?

    Look at the record of Nehemiah's behavior and words in Chapter 1. What character qualities did he possess? Why are these particular traits prerequisites for the ministry of intercession?

    What principles of intercession can we glean from Nehemiah's prayer in verses 5–11?

    What insights from Nehemiah 1 are most applicable to our relationships within this group?

    How can we keep the promise "I'll pray for you" from becoming just another church cliché?

Another approach would be to study examples of intercession in the New Testament. Examine the passages listed in the chart on page 20. Fill in the chart as you work through your study.

INTERCESSION IN THE NEW TESTAMENT

Reference	Person Prayed For	Person Praying	Aim of Prayer
Luke 22:31–32			
John 17			
Acts 4:23–31			
Acts 12:5, 12			
2 Cor. 1:11			
Eph. 1:15–21			
Eph. 3:14–19			
Eph. 6:18–19			
Phil. 1:3–11			
Col. 1:9–12			
Col. 4:3, 4			
Col. 4:12–13			
1 Tim. 2:1–4			
2 Tim. 1:3			

METHODOLOGY

It should go without saying, but I'm going to say it anyway! *Bible discussion flourishes in a class or study group where participatory methods are the norm, not the exception.*

The more consistently you involve learners, the more successful any specific attempt at discussion will be. If you pop a question out of the blue to a group accustomed to straight lecture, you'll likely receive limited responses. Yet in a class where a mix of methods is routine, what happens when you pose the same question? The room buzzes with dialogue! Involve your group members through a variety of approaches, and watch the learning atmosphere warm up.

Professional educators have investigated hundreds of classroom sessions, comparing various measures of student attitudes and outcomes with the methods employed by teachers. Their bottom-line finding reveals the value of variety in learning activities. *The more predictable one's teaching methodology, the lower the impact on students. The less predictable one's choice of learning activities, the greater the impact.*[10]

Research on high and low-rated college teachers has generated similar findings. In a study at an American university with 120 full-time faculty, the sample population consisted of ten of the eleven teachers rated highest by students and colleagues, plus ten of the twelve teachers rated lowest. Without prior notification, the researcher audio taped three seventy minute class periods for each teacher. The investigator's discoveries teem with implications for church teachers and small group leaders.

> The high-rated college teachers used interaction patterns that were noticeably different from those of the low-rated group. . . . High-rated teachers spent significantly higher portions of time in accepting student feelings and in praising and using student ideas. The proportion of time spent in student-initiated activity was significantly higher. And time devoted to lecture . . . was significantly less in the classrooms of high-rated teachers.[11]

For a particular Bible lesson, on what basis do you choose one method over another? When you sit down to plan your learning activities, what factors or guidelines should percolate in your brain? If you *always* elicit participation, how do you choose which discussion format to employ? Do you stick with a simple question-and-answer approach? When is it good to frame a session around research assignments distributed to members of the group in advance?

Choosing an appropriate study method isn't all that difficult. After praying for wisdom, consider the following seven criteria. The key words and evaluative questions will help you make good choices.

Message—What teaching methods will clearly and accurately convey the message of this Bible passage? Is the material so complex or controversial that I need to provide background, through a brief lecture, for fruitful discussion?

Environment—How does the physical environment of my class or study group affect my choice of learning activities? What techniques does the physical setting or lack of equipment eliminate? What procedures, such as dividing into smaller buzz groups, does the space or room layout prevent?

Time—What methods are realistic for the time frame I have? Should I substitute one discussion strategy for another that will conserve a few precious minutes?

Hospitality—What approaches to this lesson will help create a warm, hospitable learning atmosphere? Which discussion format will promote research in the biblical text *and* build relationships?

Objectives—Which Bible learning activities will best meet the stated lesson objectives? How can I structure the discussion to accelerate understanding of Bible truths? To enhance awareness of their practical implications?

Discovery—What methods will propel group members into the Bible passage so they can discover truths for themselves? How can my questions best highlight the most important facts and principles in the text? Do any of my questions encourage speculation rather than investigation and analysis of Bible content?

Students—In light of the number of people in my group, what teaching techniques are most appropriate? How should their ages and levels of spiritual maturity influence my choice of methods? What teaching style did previous leaders of the group employ effectively? How will the way the group was taught previously affect learners' receptivity to my teaching strategies?

Notice that the first letters of those seven key words spell out METHODS. Using these guidelines, you'll be able to select appropriate methods for leading your discussion group this week!

Assimilation

To assimilate means to absorb into a system, or into the cultural tradition of a particular group of people. Assimilation occurs in a Bible study when a visitor feels welcome and quickly shifts from marginal commitment to consistent participation in the group. How well does your group assimilate new people? Find out by answering these questions:

- *What percentage of guests attending my class or group return?*
- *How frequently do newcomers drop out after a few weeks or months?*
- *What words describe the behavior of "regulars" toward visitors?*
- *What strategies do I employ to create a sense of belonging and improve assimilation?*

After wrestling with these questions, my local church created a "class host" position for each adult Sunday school class. We recruited couples with exceptional relational skills to introduce visitors to the class, call first-time guests during the week, and to generally enhance fellowship among learners. Try adapting the following job description to your local church or revise it for the setting of your study.

CORNERSTONE CHURCH
ADULT CLASS HOSTS

Purpose—To help course participants feel welcome by establishing an atmosphere of warmth and acceptance.

Requirements—
- Evidence of genuine Christian conversion and growth
- Member of Cornerstone Church
- Regular attendance in Cornerstone's worship services

- Attend at least 80 percent of class sessions during the year
- A one-year commitment to this ministry
- Willingness to work as a team. This position will be filled by two persons, one male and one female. A married couple is preferred.

Competencies—
- A spirit of hospitality, enjoying making people feel valued and welcome
- An affinity for meeting and greeting new people
- Faithfulness in handling details and keeping records

Responsibilities—
- Learn the names of participants and call them by name each week
- Greet guests and introduce them to others in the class
- Contact every guest by phone within one week of their first visit
- Develop a class roll of regular members, including addresses and phone numbers
- Plan, promote, and implement at least one fellowship/social activity for class participants every three months. Seek to cultivate relationships and improve assimilation of guests into the life of the church.
- Coordinate weekly provision of coffee/refreshments
- Arrange for someone in the class to serve as host when you plan to be absent
- Suggest additional ways to make course participants feel welcome and improve the learning environment. Work with the class teacher to determine the nature and direction of this ministry.
- Consult with the Director of Christian Education once each quarter to evaluate progress, brainstorm ideas, and implement suggestions for improving the social climate of classes
- Consult with the teacher regularly concerning classroom fellowship activities and the amount of time devoted to host-related duties

Another concrete way to improve assimilation is to utilize creative get-acquainted or team-building strategies. Use these ideas to bridge the social distance between visitors and regulars:

Name Acrostic—Distribute name tags or 3-by-5 cards. Tell everyone to write his or her first name vertically on the left side of the tag or card.

Have each person then use each of the letters of his or her name as the first letter of a word that tells something about his or her life: personality, employment, hobbies, past experiences—you name it! For instance, in the name "Paul," "P" could stand for "promotion." "A" could refer to "area" and signify a recent move into the area. "U" could stand for "upbeat" and refer to the person's attitude. "L" could represent "loss," and refer to anything from a weight loss to the death of a loved one. Give group members time to explain their acrostics to the group. If you teach a large class, form groups of four to six people for this activity.

Nonverbal Introductions — Divide the group into pairs. Give each person two minutes to introduce himself to his or her partner—*without using words.* The partner may speak, guessing what the communicator is trying to say nonverbally. After two minutes, switch and give the other person a chance to introduce himself the same way. Next, instruct each pair to join another twosome. Then give everyone two minutes *to introduce his partner* to the new pair—nonverbally, of course. Before you reconvene, tell each foursome to exchange names and talk over their non-verbal experience. (Don't be surprised at eruptions of laughter, or delays in reassembling. Folks relish this game and the creativity it fosters.)

Optional: Use the nonverbal introductions as a springboard for a discussion of communication patterns in small groups. Ask: *What did you learn about interpersonal communication from this activity? What nonverbal messages do members of groups often send? What examples of negative nonverbal cues can you cite? What positive nonverbal cues enhance the relational climate of a group? How can awareness of each other's nonverbal messages improve our ministry to one another?*

TRANSPARENCY

Sometimes the pivot on which a good Bible discussion turns is the leader's transparency. Transparency often takes the form of sharing a personal illustration or asking learners to intercede on your behalf. What happens when you add this personal dimension to your teaching? You send positive messages to participants:

- "What we're studying has encouraged (or convicted) me."

- "This lesson has been prepared in my heart, not just in my head."
- "I'm not self-sufficient. I need to lean on Christ daily. And I need others in the body of Christ."

Genuinely identify with learners—coming across as *real*—and you've found the "open sesame" to their hearts. Thirty interviews with Bible college students unveiled to me the power of revealing personal experiences. In my doctoral dissertation research, I asked the students to describe behaviors of faculty members that improve student-faculty relationships. What they shared also applies to church and home Bible study settings. *Twenty-six out of thirty mentioned transparency as a positive teacher trait leading to nonclassroom student-teacher interaction!* Phrases such as "when a teacher shows the *down* side of himself," "when they share personal experiences," and "when an instructor talks about his own problems in daily living for God" popped up often.

One student echoed the sentiment of others when he said, "It shows that a teacher understands what I'm going through." Another respondent remembered his youth ministry professor's testimony about a time she was "disappointed with God" and didn't feel connected to Him. "I was having trouble with the same thing," he reported, "and I could relate to her and we talked about it."[12]

Even the highly respected apostle Paul modeled transparency before the people he taught: "We do not want you to be unaware, brethren, of our affliction which came to us in Asia, that we were burdened excessively, beyond our strength, so that we despaired even of life . . . we had the sentence of death within ourselves in order that we should not trust in ourselves, but in God who raises the dead. . . . He will yet deliver us, you also joining in helping us through your prayers" (2 Cor. 1:8–11).

Should a leader publicize every secret she's ever shared with God? No. Should he divulge every private sin that's ever plagued him? Of course not! Be discreet in what you say. Don't feel you have to show all your failings to the group. Before choosing what personal things to share, think about these six guidelines:

- **Will my personal anecdote accelerate Bible learning by clarifying a truth we're covering?**

- Will my personal illustration show the benefits of obeying a particular truth or the painful consequences of neglecting it?
- Will my self-revelation encourage others to share needs and prayer requests?
- Will self-disclosure meet a genuine need in my life for emotional support and prayer?
- Will my illustration portray family members or friends in a negative manner?
- Have I received permission to tell the story from people who could be embarrassed by it?

Although you should be selective in your sharing, transparency is an in-your-face slam dunk against hypocrisy and superficiality in a group. Here's how Larry Richards explains it:

Self-revelation is a *strength,* not a weakness, in spiritual leadership. The reasons for this are rooted in theology: First, we are to be examples not of perfection, but of a *process.* Second, we are to reflect the gospel. And the gospel is not "accept Christ and become perfect." The gospel is Jesus saying, "Without me you can do nothing!" (John 15:5). If we misrepresent ourselves as so "strong" that we do not need Jesus, we misrepresent the gospel of God's grace.

None of this detracts in any way from the leader's responsibility to be a good example in godliness. But it does cut us off from being hypocritical. It eliminates the need to pretend whenever we hurt. In sharing ourselves, in being *real* with others, they may well see our weaknesses . . . but they will also see *Jesus'* strength! And it will be encouraging that the transformation Jesus has been working in us can be worked in them as well![13]

The late pastor and author Ray Stedman echoes Richards' point:

Our earthiness must be as apparent to others as the power is, so they may see that the secret is *not* us, but God. That is why we must be transparent people, not hiding our weaknesses and failures, but honestly admitting them when they occur.[14]

Also strive to promote transparency among your group members. Perhaps the wisest approach is to ask for personal reactions to the Bible lesson you're covering. In any given lesson, I may employ just one or two such questions. And I reserve questions of this sort for the final minutes of a lesson. People first need Bible content to provide the grist for their thinking. Here's a list of questions that have been successful for me:

- **What personal application or carry-over idea has the Lord given you from this study?**
- **What personal reasons for praising God does this Scripture passage offer?**
- **What personal need or issue has the Holy Spirit exposed during this study? How can we pray with you about it?**
- **Who can illustrate one of our lesson truths from your personal experience?**
- **What aspect of this study encourages you most? Why?**
- **What part of this study convicts you? Why?**
- **What fresh, I-never-thought-of-that-before insight did you glean from today's Scripture?**
- **As we identified timeless truths in today's lesson, perhaps a positive role model came to mind. If so, tell us about this person. How did he or she apply or demonstrate some point we covered?**
- **What unresolved questions on this subject matter still goad you?**

ENVIRONMENT

What message does the physical environment of your meeting area convey? Do cleanliness, decor, and arrangement of chairs provide a welcome mat, or give participants the impression they weren't expected? Is the temperature too stuffy or uncomfortably cool? Does noise generated by adjacent classes or chattering kids intrude on Bible learning? Count on it: The physical surrounding dramatically affects the social climate and attitudes of a study group.

If you consistently employ discussion, and if space permits, place chairs in a pattern that facilitates group communication. A circle doesn't guarantee stimulating interaction. But staring at Bill's bald spot or counting the curls in Cathy's hair certainly doesn't expedite learning.

In a more formal context, such as a school or church classroom, try a U-shaped layout. Have learners sit around tables, and have a small table and a board for the teacher. The U-shape allows all participants to see each other and promotes interchange of ideas. The special spot for the teacher connotes authority and control. And the leader can stand for parts of the presentation, as needed. Tables also provide students a natural protection against the discomfort of the discussion process. They feel less vulnerable to peers' analysis of their ideas.

For teachers of teens, Bill McNabb and Steven Mabry advocate the "rotation principle." You'll motivate kids and spark lively discussions by periodically changing Bible study locations. Take them to an empty jail cell to launch a series on Philippians, which Paul wrote from prison. Discuss God's creativity from Genesis 1 or Psalm 8 during a midnight picnic under the stars. Or sit on the roof of the church building to discuss important biblical events that occurred on roofs: David spying on Bathsheba while she bathed (2 Samuel 11), or Peter receiving a vision that taught him to include Gentiles in God's plan of salvation (Acts 10).[15]

Whether you rotate the setting or stick to one meeting place, the physical environment is a critical variable in the learning process. Do all you can to make the meeting place conducive to discussion.

Seven words formed the organizational framework for Chapter 2. These words represent strategies for creating a group atmosphere that stimulates discussion:

C aring
L aughter
I ntercession
M ethodology
A ssimilation
T ransparency
E nvironment

The first letter of each word form an easy-to-remember acronym: **C-L-I-M-A-T-E.** You don't have to be a meteorologist to keep tabs on the climate in your study group.

CHAPTER THREE

Preparing Observation Questions

F RED SMITH—BUSINESSMAN, management consultant, and author—
burns a hole in my mind with this laser beam of truth:

> When someone says, "I don't mind standing up in front of people; prepa-
> ration is what kills me," I suspect he's not a communicator as much as he
> is an exhibitionist![1]

Ouch! That's a mince-no-words indictment of folks who love to teach,
but hate to prepare.

Smith mentions the two phases of Bible study leadership: *preparation*
and *presentation.* What you do prior to the group or class session is preparation. What you say and do during the meeting is presentation. When it
comes to the total amount of time you devote to a Bible lesson, presentation
should be just the tip of the instructional iceberg. Preparation is definitely
the more important responsibility.

Yet teachers and discussion facilitators—and even their trainers—often
concentrate on presenting a lesson at the expense of preparing it. Ever notice
how books and workshops aimed at teacher improvement focus almost
exclusively on presentation skills?

It's understandable that we channel an inordinate amount of energy
into the presentation. *Others watch us as we lead the group!* We want their
approval, or we hope to feed off their enthusiasm for learning. (If you've ever
felt that rush of adrenaline right before or during a lesson, you know what I

mean.) Conversely, spending several hours preparing doesn't boost our heart rate or stimulate our salivary glands. It's a private discipline, not a public performance. No one is around to evaluate our competency or to spur us on with kudos.

Since you're a Bible teacher, you probably yearn to be a communicator, not an exhibitionist. You're willing to pay the price of what I call "ownership" of Bible content. In the next few chapters, I'll show you how to stake a claim in a Bible passage. You'll improve your preparation of *content* by learning to observe key facts, to identify timeless truths, and to pinpoint possible applications for you and your learners. You'll enrich preparation of *methods* by discovering how to turn your observations, interpretations, and applications into stimulating questions for group discovery.

Now let's take a more microscopic look at the *observation* stage of lesson preparation.

FOCUSING ON FACTS

When it came to investigating a crime scene, the fictional character Sherlock Holmes possessed an eagle eye. That's because his creator had him honing his powers of observation in everyday situations.

One day a stranger visited Holmes' office. The detective gazed at the guest for several seconds. Then he spoke to his associate, Watson: "Beyond the obvious facts that this gentleman has at some time done manual labor, that he dips snuff, that he is a Freemason, that he has spent time in China, and that he has done a considerable amount of writing lately, I can deduce nothing else."

Watson, amazed at Holmes' capacity to deduce so many facts after such a cursory glance, later prodded his boss for an explanation. Watson wanted to know why he didn't notice the same things, because, as he told Sherlock Holmes, "I believe that my eyes are as good as yours."

"Quite so," replied the famous detective. Then Holmes put his finger on the difference between them. "You see, but you do not *observe*."[2]

The capacity to observe, not merely to see, is as important to Bible study leaders as it is to crime investigators. Timeless truths and their applications are only as sturdy as their factual foundation. On the next few pages, you'll meet an effective method for finding the facts in a Bible passage. Then you'll discover how you can plan questions that direct your learners to the most consequential details.

First, though, let's define "observation." As Sherlock Holmes indicated, it's more than just focusing your physical eyes on something; it also requires intense mental effort. *Applied to your investigation of Bible content,*

Observation **is the close inspection of a Bible passage, usually resulting in a written record and classification of facts.**

Applied to your leadership of Bible discussions,

Observation **is the group members' discovery of carefully selected facts that illustrate or support timeless truths. In a Bible discussion, probes that lead learners into the text to spot specific facts or patterns of data are** *observation questions.*

Before giving your group members observation assignments, you must first discover significant content in your own search of Scripture and then formulate questions to lead group members to find that information. Using the techniques that follow, you'll soon be creating questions that prompt factual discovery and stimulate discussion.

FINDING THE FACTS

Have you ever come across a statement that was remarkably simple, yet at the same time extremely profound? Seemingly trivial, yet full of significance? So obvious that it goes without saying—yet too momentous *not* to communicate it?

Here's a maxim that shows you what I mean:

If you are looking for something, you are more likely to find it.

Pretty self-evident, huh? Yet the statement captures a truth integral to the observation phase of Bible study. When you probe a passage, you're more apt to spot important facts if those details were on your "most wanted" list in the first place. The more intentional you are in your search of the text, the more facts you'll glean. It's necessary, then, to become familiar with *the kinds of information* that most often crop up in God's Word.

What follows is a series of "observation cues." Each is a signal to examine a Bible passage for a particular kind of factual information. To expedite your note taking during lesson preparation, you can put these clues on a chart or separate worksheet. The chart works best if you use it with no more than a Bible chapter, and no less than a single episode or long paragraph. Reproduce the headings in the text on a sheet of paper, leaving enough space for writing after each one. In most instances, your record of observations will fit on one side of the paper.

OBSERVATION CHART OF _____ (PASSAGE)

Context—
What (Passage Summary)—
Who—
Commands—
When—
Where—
Cause-Effect—
Repetitions—
Literary Features—
Contrasts—
Classifications—
Extra-Biblical Research—

One qualification is in order. Not every Bible passage contains every type of factual content on the chart. For instance, the text you're examining may not contain a command. But remember the maxim: If it *does* include a command, you'll probably notice it because you were *looking* for it!

Now let's define each kind of observation:

Context—Context refers to the discourse or action that surrounds the Bible passage you're studying. It's the larger environment into which your lesson fits. Understanding the circumstances or needs addressed in the Bible book—as well as the events surrounding your particular episode—greatly increases your capacity to understand the text.

In examining the context, you must at least answer this question: *What instructions or events immediately precede or follow this Bible passage?* Don't dig into the text until you've skimmed a few paragraphs before and after the section you're studying.

What (Passage Summary)—Write a skeletal summary of "What's happening?" (in narrative literature), or "What's the author saying?" (in instructional literature). *Keep your summary short—under fifty words—even if you're examining a long passage.* All you're after is an abbreviated synopsis of the passage.

Who—Jot down every person or group of people mentioned in the text. List all names, including supernatural beings (Christ, Holy Spirit, Satan, etc.). Include references to unnamed persons and groups, such as "my beloved brethren," or "the multitudes." To show how often a name or group appears, list every verse in which you find it.

Commands—Write a short version of every imperative. You'll encounter two types of admonitions: *Time-bound* commands, usually found in a historical narrative, require immediate follow-through in a particular situation. Jesus told a paralytic to "rise, take up your pallet and go home" (Mark 2:11). *Timeless* commands apply to the contemporary reader as well as the author's original audience. What Peter said to first-century believers is also God's directive for us: "Like the Holy One who called you, be holy yourselves also in all your behavior" (1 Peter 1:15).

When—List references to time, or the timing of events in relation to one another. Scour the text for terms such as "immediately," "after," "before sunrise," "always," and "at the first preaching of the gospel."

Where—Itemize every mention of geography or location. Include where something occurred ("in the boat," or "by the sea") as well as direct references to cities or countries ("in Thessalonica").

Cause-Effect—Look for cause-effect relationships in the text. Does the author state or imply that one thing happened as a result of another? Does he give specific counsel to readers as a direct result of something they said or did? In Philippians 1:3–5, we find that Paul's intercessory ministry for his readers was prompted by their "participation in the gospel"—a reference to their financial support of his work. Jesus' stilling of the storm caused fear within the disciples (Mark 4:41).

Repetitions—What words, phrases, behaviors, or topics surface repeatedly in the passage? What ideas, attitudes, or burdens of the author recur as you read?

Literary Features—What literary genre does the author utilize? Is it a letter? A historical narrative? A poem addressed to God? What figures of speech can you excavate from the text?

Common literary devices include *similes* and *metaphors*. A simile introduces a comparison with the word "like" or "as." (The person who meditates in God's Word "will be like a tree firmly planted by streams of water.") A metaphor *implies* likeness between two different things. ("The Lord is my shepherd," or "you are the light of the world.")

Contrasts—How did the author employ contrast to make a point or to tell his story? Keep an eye out for differences in how characters responded to Jesus or to the gospel. Look for before/after contrasts in people who encountered Christ. Notice contrasting circumstances, states of mind, behavior patterns, grammatical forms, and phraseology.

When Jesus healed ten lepers, nine hurried home with the news; only one returned to thank Him (Luke 17:11–19). A self-destructive, demon-possessed man became a winsome witness in his hometown (Mark 5:1–20). John exposed hypocrisy and self-deception by differentiating between what we *say* and what we *do* (1 John 1:6, 10; 2:4, 6, 9). And the apostle Paul drew a contrast between *anxiety* and *the peace of God* in Philippians 4:6–7.

Classifications—Examine the lists of people, commands, repetitions, and other data you've recorded. Can you systematically arrange any of those facts into categories? Can you logically lump together various pieces of information? For example, you may be able to sort people according to their responsiveness to the gospel or their ethnic/religious background. Or you might be able to classify commands on the basis of life areas covered (church, family relationships, personal disciplines—you name it!).

Extra-Biblical Research—As you search for facts in the text, you may encounter theological terms, historical allusions, controversial content, or obscure remarks. Your brain may percolate with questions about particular passage elements. When that happens, don't put aside your observation of the text to go looking for background. Instead, jot down your question or the word you want to look up. Return to it later, when it's time for extra-biblical research. The identity of "the saints . . . of Caesar's household" (Phil. 4:22) may puzzle you. Or you may question what it means to "deliver over to Satan" a wayward church member (1 Tim. 1:18–20). After your examination of the text, go to resource books and find the answers you seek.

Now that we've looked at the various kinds of factual information within a biblical text, let's look at an example of a passage studied using this method.

SAMPLE OBSERVATION CHART

Look over the following sample chart for Matthew 4:1–11. You'll see how the observation cues pull passage elements toward you like iron filings to a magnet.

OBSERVATION CHART OF MATTHEW 4:1–11

Context—This episode occurred right after Jesus' baptism at the hands of John the Baptist, & the Father's affirmation of the Son (Mt. 3:13–17). It immediately preceded the launch of His public ministry, and appointment of the inner core of disciples (Mt. 4:12–25).

What (Passage Summary)—The Spirit led Jesus into wilderness. Jesus fasted 40d/n. Satan appeared w/ 3 temptations; 1-turn stones to bread (3); 2-jump from pinnacle of temple in Jerusalem (5–6); 3-worship Satan for control over earth's kingdoms (8–9), Jesus resisted ea. w/ quote from OT, then Satan fled.

Who—Jesus (1, 7, 10) (pronoun other verses); the Spirit (1); devil (1, 5, 8, 11); tempter (3); Son of God (3, 6); Man (4); God (4); angels (6, 11); the Lord your God (7, 10); Satan (10).

Commands—"Command that these stones become bread" (3); "Throw yourself down" (6); "You shall not put the Lord your God to the test" (7); "Begone, Satan!"(10); "You shall worship the Lord Your God, and serve Him only" (10).

When—After He had fasted 40 days and 40 nights, then He was hungry (2); Angels ministered to Jesus after the devil left Him (11).

Where—In the wilderness (1); the mouth of God (4); into the holy city (5); on the pinnacle of the temple (5); throw yourself down (6); on their hands (angels will bear you up) (6); to a high mountain (8); kingdoms of the world (8); fall down (& worship) (9).

Cause-Effect—40 day fast caused hunger (2); "If you worship me, I'll give you kingdoms of world" (8, 9); Jesus: "Be gone, Satan" (cause v.10); devil left him (effect v. 11).

Repetitions—"It is written" Jesus (4, 7, 10); devil (6); "If you are the Son of God" (3, 6); angels (6, 11); "The Lord your God" (7, 10); Tempt (test) (1, 3, 7); Satan 3 temptations, not one or two; Worship (9, 10).

Literary Features—Genre: historical narrative containing dialog between main characters; the mouth of God (4).

Contrasts—Led by Spirit, yet tempted by devil (1); contrast between "spiritual highs" of baptism & miraculous affirmation by Father (Mt. 3) & the private battle with Satan in wilderness (4:1–11); Worship Satan (9) vs. worship God (10); devil left, angels came.

Classifications—Groupings of people: 1) Godhead: Jesus (Son of God), the Spirit, the Lord Your God, the Father (ch. 3 context); 2) Satanic: the devil, tempter, Satan; 3) Angels.

Extra-Biblical Research—?Source of 3 verses Jesus quoted and one Satan quoted; If you are Son of God—Did Satan doubt this or want Jesus to doubt it? How else can it be translated?

In the section that follows, you'll discover what to do with all this information. You'll learn how to prepare observation assignments that lead learners to important discoveries in the passage.

Formulating Factual Questions

It's important that your group members also be familiar with the facts in your passage. So observing the text must be an integral part of your group time. But don't make everyone fill out an observation chart every time you meet!

From the details you've stockpiled, select bits of information most integral to interpretation and application. Sift through the passage elements and separate the most important from the less important. This *selectivity* phase of your preparation is crucial. Bruce Wilkinson, author of *The Seven Laws of the Learner,* says:

> Believe it or not, not all facts are created equal. . . . great teachers are as skilled at knowing what should be excluded as what should be included. . . . your task is to identify those facts your students must know in order to say they truly "know" the subject. I call this group of facts the "Irreducible Minimum"—the smallest unit of information necessary for a given class to gain acceptable understanding of a given subject.[3]

When you've located the most important information, you're ready to formulate questions for group discussion. *Observation questions are probes that lead learners into the text to spot specific facts or patterns of data.* Three guidelines govern my development of observation questions. I pose such questions to preview the passage, to point out trends or patterns in the data, and to construct sturdy support for timeless truths. In the sections that follow, we're going to take a closer look at those types of questions.

To Preview the Passage

Near the beginning of a Bible discussion, I often ask questions that bring out essential information that require learners to grasp the outstanding events or strains of thought. I may want people to draw a bead on the major characters and episodes, to notice the primary line of reasoning in a discourse, or to condense the author's advice. What I write in the "What (Passage Summary)" part of the observation chart usually provides content for those questions.

Examples from Matthew 4:1–11:

What specific temptations did Satan fling at Jesus?
What events transpired right before and after Jesus' dialog with Satan?

To Pinpoint Patterns

You want your learners to absorb the basic facts, yet *excessive* reliance on observation questions creates a hazard. Never ask a question that's too obvious to everyone. Such inquiries can seem insulting.

To increase the challenge in factual assignments given to group members, *focus on a thread of related details woven throughout a Bible passage.* Your questions should require learners to scan several verses and locate multiple answers. A question should rarely require people to parrot back a phrase from a single verse. Probes that escort learners through several verses stimulate them far more than factual questions rooted in a single verse. Sometimes the repetitions, the list of characters, and your classification of factual material will reveal patterns or connectedness among the facts. Then your questions can zero in on those connections.

EXAMPLES FROM MATTHEW 4:1–11

What did Jesus' responses to the three temptations have in common?
How would you group or classify the personalities or cast of characters mentioned in the passage?

A chapter-length lesson offers extended opportunities to examine trends in the text. Mark 5 is a great example. Jesus exorcised a legion of demons from a man (vv. 1–20), stopped the hemorrhaging in a desperate woman (vv. 25–34), and raised Jairus' daughter from the dead (vv. 21–24, 35–43). Notice how answering the following questions requires the reading of numerous verses, not just one.

According to verses 1–5, what were the effects of demon-possession on the man?
What words or phrases in verses 6–13 show Jesus' superiority over the demons?
What did the three individuals who encountered Jesus have in common?
How did the demoniac, Jairus, and the woman initially approach Jesus?

TO INFORM INTERPRETATION

In the next chapter, we'll examine how to move from observation (what a passage says) to interpretation (what a passage means). For now, let's just say that facts provide the fertile soil in which principles for living and timeless truths grow. Use the following questions to help you decide which facts to cover with your group:

Which passage elements trigger thoughts that lead you to analysis and interpretation? What factual information gives credibility to your conclusions? What are the facts that hatch the truths you plan to emphasize?

The details that support an interpretation may reside in a single sentence, or may constitute a thread of information spread over several verses. In the following examples I'll add an analytical question as follow-up to each factual probe. These sets of questions demonstrate the link between observation and interpretation.

MATTHEW 4:1–11

Observation—In His reaction to the temptations, what words or phrase did Jesus repeatedly use?
Interpretation—What truth about handling temptation did Jesus model for us?
Observation—What were Jesus' circumstances *immediately preceding* Satan's first temptation?
Interpretation—What does Jesus' physical hunger, combined with the nature of the first temptation, teach us about Satan's strategy?

MARK 5

Observation—According to verses 1–5, what were the effects of demon-possession on the man?
Interpretation—What do these effects illustrate about Satan and his purposes in relation to us?

✳︎ ✳︎ ✳︎

To review, let's trace the steps you've taken through this chapter. You've defined the observation phase of Bible study and identified the kinds of facts to look for in a passage. You've also received a method for recording and categorizing the factual information. After that, you examined criteria for determining which facts to cover with your group and viewed sample questions that catapult learners into the text to find the key facts.

I must, however, offer the following disclaimer: *Posing observation questions isn't the only way to cover necessary factual content.* If you're pressed for time, save a couple of minutes by presenting the foundational facts in a lecture. Then concentrate on involving learners in the interpretation and application segments of the Bible lesson.

To illustrate what I mean, let's return to the questions from Mark 5 in this "To Inform Interpretation" section of the chapter.

I posed two questions showing the link between observation and interpretation:

> According to verses 1–5, what were the effects of demon-possession on the man?
> What do these effects illustrate about Satan and his purpose in relation to us?

Instead, you could summarize the relevant data for your group, then ask just the analytical question:

> The demoniac was a social outcast who lived among the tombs. Night and day, folks heard his piercing screams as he roamed the countryside and gashed himself with stones. What do these circumstances illustrate about Satan and his purpose in relation to us?

Or you might decide that the material is too self-evident to deserve restatement. Perhaps the reading required for the interpretation question pinpoints all the data needed for analysis. If that's the case, merely formulate the analytical question to demonstrate its basis in fact:

> What do the effects of demon-possession in verses 1–5 teach us about Satan and his purposes in relation to mankind?

Finding the facts in a Bible passage is simply the means to a nobler end, never the purpose of the pursuit. Now we're going to move from mastery of minutia to interpretation of information. The next chapter will stimulate your investigative blood by showing you how to analyze what you've so carefully observed in Scripture.

CHAPTER FOUR

PREPARING
INTERPRETATION QUESTIONS

T HROUGH OUR CHURCHES we work long and hard to effectively convey the gospel to a needy world. But it seems we aren't as effective when communicating within our own ranks. Someone culled the following announcements from various church bulletins and newsletters. Notice how an inadvertent placement or omission of words permits an errant interpretation.

- *During the absence of our pastor, we enjoyed the rare privilege of hearing a good sermon when J. F. Stubbs supplied our pulpit.*
- *The Rev. Merriwether spoke briefly, much to the delight of the audience.*
- *For those of you who have children and don't know it, we have a nursery downstairs.*
- *The pastor will preach his farewell message, after which the choir will sing, "Break Forth Into Joy."*
- *Don't let worry kill you off—let the church help.*
- *The eighth graders will be presenting Shakespeare's "Hamlet" in the church basement on Friday at 7 p.m. The congregation is invited to attend this tragedy.*
- *The ladies of the church have cast off clothing of every kind, and they can be seen in the church basement Friday afternoon.*
- *This afternoon there will be a meeting in the south and north ends of the church. Children will be baptized at both ends.*
- *Remember in prayer the many who are sick of our church and community.*

- *Today's sermon: "How Much Can a Man Drink?" with hymns from a full choir.*
- *Sermon title: "The Role of Women in the Church." Closing hymn: "Rise Up, O Men of God!"* [1]

How's that for lifting announcements from the blandly literal to the sublimely absurd?

Transferring a message from one person's mind to a different mental receptacle is sometimes a precarious process. Incorrectly interpreting someone else's words can be humorous, but when it comes to Bible study and teaching, accurate interpretation is essential. What we're after is meaning, not just factual information.

In this chapter I'll define "interpretation" and suggest ways to reach conclusions by analyzing available information. I'll also furnish examples of appropriate interpretations and demonstrate how to ask analytical questions that stimulate learners' investigation of the text.

This analytical phase of your personal Bible study and teaching can seem complex. But I'm confident that you can learn from it to improve your Bible discussions. God does a whole lot better job of communicating than some church secretaries!

INTRODUCING INTERPRETATION

The three basic steps to personal Bible study are also distinct phases of discussion leadership:

Observation—What does the passage *say?*

Interpretation—What does the passage *mean?*

Application—What is the *significance* of the passage for our lives?

In Chapter 3 you read about the observation stage. When you study God's Word,

---

Observation **is the close inspection of a Bible passage, usually resulting in a written record and classification of facts.**

When you teach a group,

Observation is group members' discovery of carefully
selected facts that illustrate or support timeless truths.
In a Bible discussion, probes that lead learners into
the text to spot specific facts or patterns of data are
observation questions.

Now the spotlight shifts to *interpretation*. When you analyze the details
of a Bible passage, you become an interpreter. You interpret when you seek to
derive timeless truths or principles for living from the story, instructions, or
discourse under consideration. Solid interpretation requires a careful process
that's satisfied with nothing less than God-intended conclusions supported
by the facts. According to Hans Finzel, author of *Observe Interpret Apply,*

> *Interpretation* is the step where you pull all the facts together into a coher-
> ent explanation of their meaning. . . . To illustrate the process, let's use
> the example of buying a car. You have studied the car carefully, kicked the
> tires, poked under the hood, taken it for a drive, and even had a
> mechanic look it over. You've gathered all the facts. You conclude that it's
> a bad investment because the facts indicate the car is a lemon. That's
> interpretation — determining the meaning once all the facts are in. . . .
> Interpretation is built on thorough observation.[2]

When you study a Bible passage,

Interpretation is your identification of timeless truths
implied or illustrated by passage content.

Applied to your leadership of Bible discussions,

Interpretation is the learners' acquisition of timeless
truths as a direct result of textual analysis. Probes that
spur learners to mull over the meaning suggested
by selected facts are *interpretation questions.*

RESTRICTING THE RANGE

On the library shelves of any seminary sit scores of books treating Bible interpretation with microscopic scrutiny. But we can't go too deeply into that process in this chapter. So I'm providing a simple procedure for analyzing information in a Bible passage. Following my suggestions may not furnish everything you want to know about a section of Scripture, but it will help you discover truths on your own before you consult the experts.

SIMPLIFYING THE STEPS

As you work through this process of interpretation, you'll want to implement the following steps in succession. Begin this process only after you've read your Bible passage several times and cataloged information from it.

Prayer—The Holy Spirit who inspired Scripture is the same Person who illuminates its meaning. He sheds light on passages that otherwise leave us in the dark. Jesus promised, "When He, the Spirit of truth, comes, He will guide you into all the truth" (John 16:13). Jesus' words may have carried special meaning for the original disciples, but the apostle Paul implied that the Holy Spirit serves as a Bible interpreter for *all* believers:

> No one knows the thoughts of God except the Spirit of God. We have not received the spirit of the world but the Spirit who is from God, that we may understand what God has freely given us. . . . The man without the Spirit does not accept the things that come from the Spirit of God, for they are foolishness to him, and he cannot understand them, because they are spiritually discerned (1 Cor. 2:11–12, 14 NIV).

When we realize our need for illumination, we remember to pray as we study a Bible passage. With a spirit of humility and dependence, we ask the Lord to clarify timeless truths in the text. When we're stumped, we implore Him to open mental locks. We adopt the teachable spirit reflected in the Psalmist's prayer: "Open my eyes, that I may behold wonderful things from Thy Law" (Ps. 119:18).

"An Interpreter's Prayer" reflects a humble attitude with which to jump-start your lesson preparation. Pray it yourself as you begin. Then when your group meets, change the first person singular pronouns (*I, my, me*) to plural pronouns (*we, our, us*) and read through the prayer together as a corporate expression of your reliance on God's Spirit.

INTERPRETER'S PRAYER

Father, as I study this passage, I acknowledge my need of Your Spirit's illumination. I want to glean from Your Word what You originally intended for me to receive. Nothing more . . . but nothing less! So crystallize my thinking. Show me precisely what You are saying or illustrating with all the passage elements. Don't allow my preconceived notions or personal experiences to usurp the authority of the text itself. I ask this because I want to know You better, and serve you more faithfully. Amen.

Probes—I'd like to give you a "no-sweat" set of directions, a works-like-a-charm-every-time procedure to expedite your analysis of Scripture, but that's unrealistic. The mental gymnastics are too complicated for a patented approach. Besides, the calibration in every human brain is set differently.

However, there's one thing I can say with assurance: *Interpreting God's Word requires the cultivation of curiosity.* As you develop that curiosity, your mind will begin to ask a rapid-fire barrage of questions about the passage. Drop the welcome mat to any inquiries within your mind that seek the significance of biblical information.

Remember: God's truth is objective reality. The process of probing for meaning doesn't "create" truth in any sense. Instead, it's a way to discover what God says through the facts of the text. So after you've prayed for illumination, pry open the passage with probes of all kinds. Since the same series of questions won't unlock every Bible passage, the best way to explain this investigative process is to demonstrate it.

I've hoisted observations from two historical narratives, plus a discourse from Deuteronomy. For each passage, you'll see the questions that percolate in my mind as I seek to understand the material. Perhaps this peek at my probes will serve as a catalyst for your own analysis of Bible passages.

MATTHEW 4:1–11

Observation—In response to all three temptations, Jesus quoted Scripture. He started each rebuttal with the words, "It is written."

Probes—So What? What's the significance of this repetition? Did His Scripture quotations work? Did Satan withdraw that particular temptation whenever Jesus quoted Scripture? If so, what does that say about the power of God's Word? How does the content of the Old Testament verses Jesus used relate to the content of each temptation? Or did He just pluck any verse out of His memory bank? What insight about temptation is being illustrated here? What is God saying to the contemporary reader about succeeding in spiritual warfare?

MATTHEW 4:1–11

Observation—Satan tempted Jesus three times, not just once. When Jesus rebuffed the first and second temptations, Satan retaliated with a different lure.
Probes—So What? Is this fact important? Why or why not? Why didn't the devil give up after the first rebuttal? (After all, he knew he was dealing with the Son of God!) Does this repetition lead logically to any conclusions? What does it reveal about Satan? Anything I need to know in light of the spiritual warfare that *I* face?

MARK 5:1–20

Observation—The demon-possessed man "ran up and bowed down" before Jesus (vs. 6). Jesus had been ordering the unclean spirit to leave the man, so the man said, "I implore You by God, do not torment me!" (vv. 7–8). According to verse 10, the unclean spirit "began to entreat Him earnestly not to send them out of the country." The demons "entreated Him" to send them into the swine, and Jesus "gave them permission" (vv. 12–13). Jesus exorcised the legion of demons from the man, who later "began to proclaim in Decapolis what great things Jesus had done for him" (vs. 20).
Probes—What truths is God revealing through this story? Why did the possessed man bow down before Jesus? Why did the demons resort to begging in their dialog with Jesus? What do the phrases "I implore You" (vs. 7), "began to entreat Him earnestly" (vs. 10), "entreated Him" (vs. 12),

and "He gave them permission" (vs. 13) say about Satan and his cohorts? What does this dialog and action demonstrate about Jesus?

DEUTERONOMY 6:1-9

This is an excerpt from a sermon Moses delivered before the children of Israel entered the Promised Land. He's addressing adults, concerned that their offspring adhere to the Law and adopt its value system. Many pastors use this passage when preaching on parental responsibility.

Observation — The passage teems with commands concerning the people's relationship with God, His Law, and their children. Referring to his own instructions, Moses told his listeners to "do them" (vs. 1), to "listen and be careful to do it" (vs. 3) so that "you and your son and your grandson might fear the LORD your God, to keep all His statutes, and His commandments" (vs. 2). Then he gave more specific admonitions:

- "You shall love the LORD your God with all your heart and with all your soul and with all your might" (vs. 5).
- "These words, which I am commanding you today, shall be on your heart" (vs. 6).
- "You shall teach them diligently to your sons and shall talk of them when you sit in your house and when you walk by the way and when you lie down and when you rise up" (vs. 7).

Probes—Is this just a historical record of an ancient sermon? Or is God saying something important to parents of all generations about passing on the faith? Why did the Holy Spirit inspire this particular part of Moses' sermon? To what extent are these commands timeless rather than time bound?

From these imperatives, what transferable insights about influencing children can I glean? How would I summarize the different responsibilities of parents mentioned here? And what about their order? Is there significance to their placement or sequence in the passage? How would I describe the kind of parental teaching called for in verses 7-9? What are some prerequisites for fulfilling this kind of instruction in the home?

Remember . . . *your* analysis of these Bible passages won't generate questions identical to mine. That's okay, so long as you ask the Lord to guide your analysis. So long as you strive for meaning, not just facts. So long as you cultivate a mindset willing to relocate from the comfortable confines of "observation" to the more demanding domain of "interpretation."

Precepts—The purpose of probing is to identify universal truths, which I'll call precepts. Not all the questions you ask will result in identification of truths. You'll conclude that some of the facts you scrutinize don't contain significant meaning, and the answers to some of your questions will require extra-biblical research. But your prayerful examination of factual material should begin to spawn interpretations. *The very process of posing the questions will often unveil insights that an uninquisitive mind would miss.*

When a mental light bulb comes on and you spot an insight implied by the text, summarize your conclusion in one or two sentences. Trim the fat off your thinking and refine your idea until the point stands out with clarity, accuracy, and simplicity.

The paragraphs that follow are the fruit of my analysis of Matthew 4, Mark 5, and Deuteronomy 6. You'll notice that formulating these particular precepts didn't require the wisdom of Solomon. Yet their simplicity illustrates how timeless insights stem from factual information. Though the insights aren't directly stated by the authors, you or any other conscientious Bible teacher can deduce them from the facts.

MATTHEW 4:1–11

(1) Jesus' quotation of Old Testament verses in response to each temptation demonstrates a precept about spiritual warfare: *A working knowledge of God's Word is an effective defense against temptation to sin.*

(2) That Satan tempted Jesus three times, not just once, suggests the following insight: *In his attempts to derail God's purposes and defeat God's people, Satan is persistent.*

MARK 5:1–20

The demons' servile behavior and compliance with Jesus' command to leave the man express a universal truth: *Jesus' power and authority is greater than Satan's.*

DEUTERONOMY 6:1–9

The placement, content, and correlation of Moses' commands to the adult generation of Israel implies an important truth about influencing our children in the faith: *Parents' spiritual training of children cannot be divorced from their own walk with God. Persistent and timely teaching of children stems from and depends on parents' love relationship with God and their heartfelt knowledge of His Word.*

Proofs—After you've penned conclusions from a Bible passage, try to substantiate their reliability. You can't prove their accuracy in a scientific sense, but you may find evidence to bolster their trustworthiness. As you seek to confirm the precepts you found, you must acknowledge your limitations as an interpreter, concede your need for accountability as a communicator of truth, and accept the following point: "Interpretive statements are less objectively verifiable. Their value is judged not by strict and objective standards of accuracy, but in terms of how much they illumine or how well they explain or fit the details of a passage." [3]

You'll want to fortify your findings with both *internal* and *external* information. *Internal* information is that found within Scripture. *External* information involves insights gleaned from published material about the Bible.

The most important internal support stems from the Bible passage you're studying. *What words or actions in the text serve as a basis for your interpretive statements?* Can you point to a pattern of data, a particular remark, or a character's specific course of action that undergirds your conclusion? My precepts from Matthew 4, Mark 5, and Deuteronomy 6 rest firmly on repetition of actions, behavioral patterns, and the correlation of commands within the passages. The more thoroughly you *observe* a text, the more correctly you'll interpret it. If you treat the observation phase of Bible study casually, you'll be less likely to correctly interpret the text.

A second kind of internal check involves the total teaching of Scripture on the point of your interpretive statement. Ask yourself: *Does the treatment of this topic elsewhere in Scripture corroborate my conclusion?*

Remember a basic axiom of biblical interpretation: *Scripture cannot contradict itself.* If your interpretation appears to contradict another part of Scripture, perhaps your analysis is askew. But you may also discover a logical explanation and no discrepancy after all. Expand your understanding with a reference book such as Archer's *Encyclopedia of Bible Difficulties*,[4] or Richards' *Bible Difficulties Solved*.[5]

Conversely, if other sections of Scripture clearly teach the same truth that you gleaned from your passage, you probably interpreted it correctly. Another principle of Bible interpretation should be forming in your mind: *A broad knowledge of Scripture enhances one's ability to interpret any single passage.*

Once you've done the internal research, you may want to look at external sources. If you're feeling insecure about your analysis, or the internal support for a point appears flimsy, crack open a commentary on your passage. If you're an inexperienced student of Scripture, checking your own analysis with a reference book is particularly important. Here's the question you want answered: *Does my precept dovetail with expert opinion on these verses?*

One more reason for keeping extra-biblical resources handy is to help you examine grammatical construction, historical background, or contextual details that aren't accessible through the observation method. The whole point of this chapter is to equip you and your learners to discover God's truths on your own. But you'll want to supplement your findings with those of scholars who've made it a vocation to wrestle with biblical texts.

Using the steps we've just examined to interpret a Bible passage is only part of your calling as a Bible study leader. Even more important is the task of leading group members to analyze and interpret God's Word *during group meetings*. When you prepare questions that spark *others'* analyses and interpretations of the text, you maximize the effectiveness of your time together.

GUIDING YOUR GROUP

As a Bible discussion leader, you're a *guide* to learning. You've dug into the text and uncovered treasure in the form of truth. Now it's your privilege to lead others on an expedition into God's Word. You could just dole out some of the riches you found, but you're too sharp to take that route. You realize people are more likely to cherish and to keep nuggets of truth when they do their own digging.

That's where interpretation questions enter the picture. Posing sound analytical questions is like handing learners picks and shovels. Your queries equip them to discover insights located just beneath the surface.

Digest the following checklist for interpretation questions. These guidelines will help you evaluate each probe you prepare. A good question will muster a "yes" on each of the queries.

- *Can participants point to specific passage elements to support their answer?* (Meaning stems from what the passage *says*, not from speculation.)
- *Does my question require people to explain the meaning implied or illustrated by the facts?* (If participants can answer the question just by reiterating what the text *says*, it's an observation question, not an interpretive one.)
- *Can group members answer correctly by sticking to the information provided in this Bible passage?* (Don't ask questions requiring historical background or doctrinal discernment that's outside the scope of the Bible text. If understanding your text requires that sort of material, lecture on it before discussing the questions.)
- *Does the wording of the question keep the spotlight on the Bible passage rather than on personal opinion?* (Don't allow *"What does this verse mean to you?"* to masquerade as an interpretation question. Group leaders frequently launch the interpretation phase of lessons with such a question. But this terminology often results in subjective meandering rather than textual investigation.)
- *Is the answer to this question a weighty conclusion?* (In view of time limitations and group characteristics, covering every truth in your Bible passage isn't always realistic. Shoot for interpretations that best correlate with the passage's main theme and have the greatest application potential.)

Asking these questions will help you think through the purpose and potential of each probe you're considering, and will enable you to weed out questions that might be ineffective. With these guidelines you should be well-equipped for developing solid interpretation questions. But if you're looking for more help, don't be dismayed. We're going to take an even closer look at formulating clear, accurate, sensitive, and thought-provoking questions in Chapter 7, "Guidelines for Effective Questions."

Now let's look at the precepts previously identified in this chapter. Here are questions I'd use to facilitate learners' discovery of the truths. The factual support has been summarized before each question.

MATTHEW 4:11

Precept—A working knowledge of God's Word is an effective defense against temptation.
Factual Support—In response to all three temptations, Jesus quoted Scripture. He started each rebuttal with the words, "It is written."
Interpretation Question—*What did Jesus model for us about handling temptation?*

Precept—In his attempts to derail God's purposes and defeat God's people, Satan is persistent.
Factual Support—Satan tempted Jesus three times, not just once. When Jesus rebuffed the first and second temptation, Satan retaliated with a different lure.
Interpretation Question—*What does the number of temptations flung at Jesus teach us about Satan?*

MARK 5:1–20

Precept—Jesus' power and authority are greater than Satan's.
Factual Support—The demon-possessed man "ran up and bowed down" before Jesus (vs. 6). Jesus had been ordering the unclean spirit to leave the man, so the man said, "I implore You by God, do not torment me!" (vv. 7–8). According to verse 10, the unclean spirit "began to entreat Him earnestly not to send them out of the country." The demons "entreated Him" to send them into the swine, and Jesus "gave them permission" (vv. 12–13). Jesus exorcised the legion of demons from the man, who later "began to proclaim in Decapolis what great things Jesus had done for him" (vs. 20).
Interpretation Question—*What can we learn about Jesus from His encounter with the legion of demons?*

DEUTERONOMY 6:1–9

Precept—Parents' spiritual training of children cannot be divorced from their own walk with God. Persistent and timely teaching of children stems from and depends on parents' love relationship with God, and their heart-felt knowledge of His Word.

Factual Support—After exhorting his listeners to obey all the divine instruction he was about to tell them, Moses gave the following commands:

- *"You shall love the LORD your God* with all your heart and with all your soul and with all your might"* (vs. 5).
- *"These words,* which I am commanding you today, *shall be on your heart"* (vs. 6).
- *"You shall teach them diligently to your sons* and shall talk of them when you sit in your house and when you walk by the way and when you lie down and when you rise up"* (vs. 7).

Interpretation Questions—(I'd employ a series of probes leading up to the precept. I've included succinct answers to reveal my line of reasoning.)

- *How would you describe the kind of parental teaching called for in verse 7?* (Persistent, spontaneous, informal, responsive-to-the-teachable-moment kind of instruction.)
- *What is significant about the placement, or sequence, of these commands?* (The command to nurture children *follows* admonitions to love the Lord and soak up His Word.)
- *From the content and correlation of these commands, what can we conclude about influencing the faith of our children?* (See the precept.)

In Chapter 3 we discussed how to find important facts and formulate observation questions. In this chapter we've tackled the ticklish topic of interpretation and studied sample questions that compel learners to analyze content. By now you are equipped to develop top-notch questions to lead your group in observation and interpretation of a Bible passage.

This leads us to the final phase in Bible study: application. *How can you improve your ability to discern a truth's practical implications? What constitutes teaching that changes lives? What type of questions help group members evaluate their lives in light of God's truth?*

Chapter 5 addresses these questions.

Preparing Application Questions

HEN HIS FOUR-YEAR-OLD BOY attends the first day of kindergarten, Rick won't see him off. When his infant daughter takes her first wobbly step, Rick won't snap a picture. Rick's wife moved out of state with the kids after she filed for divorce. She'd been unable feed them properly because Rick gambled away most paychecks. After the split, Rick's tardiness cost him his job, and his drunk driving totaled his Nissan. Disgruntled creditors regularly harass him over unpaid bills.

You can multiply Rick's story by tens of thousands, but if you'd known him as a teen, you'd have predicted a brighter future. His quick wit and cheerful personality endeared folks to him. Beginning in the sixth grade, Rick attended church services every Sunday for six straight years. And when it came to knowing the Bible, he wielded a swift sword.

Rick's senior high group often competed with other churches in old-fashioned Bible drills. A leader would announce a reference, and the first person to find the verse and read it aloud won a point for his team. Rick's fingers were a blur as he flipped to obscure verses in Leviticus and Zechariah. He could recite scores of Bible verses, and when he answered questions about Bible stories, you'd swear he'd been an eyewitness to the events.

But all that head knowledge didn't mean much because it didn't permeate Rick's heart. Rick didn't act much like a Christian when the church crowd wasn't around. And after moving away to college, he chucked his parents' conservative standards. He operated as if he didn't want to offend the devil.

Rick's story teaches us that a person can learn God's Word on a variety of levels. *Rote knowledge* of Scripture involves simply repeating it from memory without regard for meaning—wearing it like a new overcoat, but discarding it when it gets uncomfortable. Then there's the *comprehension* level: understanding the timeless truths stemming from Scripture and correlating them with other ideas, but never acting on them. Finally, there's the *changed-life* level: discerning how a truth should impact life, then obeying it. A lot of Rick's learning was rote. What he comprehended never resulted in life change.

These three learning levels correlate well with the three phases of Bible study and teaching covered in this book: *observation, interpretation,* and *application.* First, you extract the important facts from a passage. Then you switch to analysis and identify truths implied or illustrated by the facts. Next, you ponder the practical implications for your life and adjust your attitudes, values, and behavior accordingly.

The previous chapters have given you tools for finding facts, formulating precepts, and writing questions for the first two phases of group Bible study. Now the spotlight shifts to the ultimate purpose of Bible discussions: *transformation.* As a Bible study leader, you want to lead your study group to the highest level of learning. To help you do that, this chapter takes a close look at how to connect a truth with daily life.

Remember Rick's perfect church attendance as a teen? If his youth leader had scuttled the Bible drills and concentrated on helping Rick apply the Bible to his life, would the script to Rick's life now read differently? Who knows . . . But for all the Ricks and Rhondas in *your* group, the script is still being written.

LINK LESSONS TO LIFE

Your *study* of God's Word has three basic phases:

Observation is the close inspection of a Bible passage, usually resulting in a written record and classification of facts.

Interpretation is your identification of timeless truths
implied or illustrated by passage content.

What's distinctive about the last phase?

Application is obedience to God's truth stemming from
your awareness of its practical implications for your
attitudes and lifestyle.

Similarly, your *teaching* of God's Word should be marked by three distinguishable stages.

Observation is group members' discovery of carefully
selected facts that illustrate or support timeless truths.
In a Bible discussion, probes that lead learners into the
text to spot specific facts or patterns of data are
observation questions.

Interpretation is the learners' acquisition of timeless
truths as a direct result of their textual analysis. Probes
that spur them to mull over the meaning suggested by
selected facts are *interpretation questions.*

Application is the joint effort to identify attitude and
lifestyle changes that spring logically from Bible truths.
Together, you ponder how God's truth should affect
participants' priorities, emotions, decisions, and
relationships. Probes that prompt participants to link a
lesson to life are *application questions.*

Since *application* refers to participants' *responses* to God's Word, the
group meeting isn't usually the setting where obedience occurs. After group

members disperse, they choose to heed or to ignore the Spirit's directions. When the Holy Spirit points out a needed change, common contexts for such changes include people's homes, schools, and the marketplace.

That's why "teaching for application" doesn't refer to the attitude or behavior change itself. Instead, it's the guided process of helping learners identify follow-through possibilities. You can't guarantee that anyone will obey God's Word, but you can reserve group time to probe a passage's practical implications. You *can* make sure people leave with application scenarios percolating in their minds.

To connect Bible content to slice-of-life situations, try implementing this five-step approach to application.

Step 1: Personalize the Passage—During observation and interpretation phases, you and your group sift through God's Word. During application, *God's Word sifts through you and your group.*

Graze on that sequence: *you* first, then the people you lead. It's the same progression Paul emphasized in 1 Timothy 4:16: "Pay close attention to yourself and to your teaching." To optimize the impact of a lesson on others, first filter it through your own heart.

As you study the text, keep your antenna up for insights that bear directly upon your needs and behavior patterns. Forge a link between passage elements and situations you typically face. One way to personalize the passage is to approach it devotionally a few days before the group session. As you read, accelerate your personal application by posing the following questions:

- *How does this passage increase my appreciation for God the Father, Jesus Christ, or the Holy Spirit?*
- *What reasons for praising the Lord does the text offer?*
- *What sin to avoid or to forsake does the content expose?*
- *What positive course of action does the passage propose?*
- *What bearing do these verses have upon my prayer life?*
- *What encourages me from the passage? Why?*
- *What circumstances, decisions, or people come to mind as I read? Why?*

Questions of that sort funnel truth to your heart, not just your head. Before it becomes a lens through which you view your group, the Bible passage must become a mirror in which you see yourself. When a truth touches you, you communicate it with more passion. You speak with more enthusiasm because you're convinced the passage is potent.

Also, questions that pry open *your* heart and reveal practical implications for *you* can have the same effect on your learners. Did you find reasons for praise and encouragement in the text? So can your group members! Did you spot an association between a verse and your prayer life? So can they! The most productive devotional questions will also work well during the group meeting. Find room for them in your discussion plan.

Step 2: Connect Content to Contexts—Next, connect lesson content to group members' daily contexts for living. As you prepare, keep one eye on the Bible passage and one eye on people's characteristics, needs, and day-to-day responsibilities. The following questions help me think in terms of learner application:

- *What relationship does this principle have to my group members?*
- *What roles, relationships, and responsibilities serve as contexts for their application of this lesson?*
- *In view of my group members' life situations, what hindrances to application will they likely face?*
- *What kind of assistance or support system could help them apply this lesson?*
- *If participants heed this lesson, what positive effect will it have on their attitudes? Their decisions? Their schedules?*
- *If people ignore the passage's implication for their lives, what negative consequences will they experience?*
- *When the group meets, how can I illustrate the benefits of obeying this passage or the painful outcome of ignoring it?*

In *The Seven Laws of the Learner,* Bruce Wilkinson agrees that teaching for life change requires envisioning the potential effects of a lesson:

Help your students "see" themselves doing the principle. . . . Picture the principle in action. One reason so few people experience life change is that the teacher never helped them to see the life change occurring. . . .

Picture the principle in action in different settings and circumstances. . . . Grip your students with the overpowering benefits bestowed
upon those who embrace the principle. Shock your students with the tragic
consequences of those who reject it.[1]

Wilkinson urges leaders to "picture the principle in action" during the
group session. But heeding his appeal requires you to ask yourself life-related
questions long before your group gathers. When you contemplate application contexts prior to the meeting, you'll be more prepared to present them
effectively during the meeting.

Step 3: Ask for Anecdotes—You've applied the Bible lesson to your
own life. You've thought through its potential effect on your group members. The third step in teaching for application is to plan questions that
draw out personal examples from participants. Ask them to provide scenarios for application. Let their experiences convey the benefits of obeying a
truth, or the consequences of ignoring it. Personal questions catapult people
from the comprehension level of learning to the changed-life level. They're
compelled to think about a truth's relationship to their lives.

Allow me to demonstrate from the three Bible passages examined in
previous chapters.

MATTHEW 4:1–11

You've covered the following precept about spiritual warfare: *A working knowledge of God's Word is an effective defense against temptation
to sin.*

To help them picture this principle in action, ask: *Who can give an example
of the power of God's Word to defend against temptation?*

MARK 5:1–20

The demon's servile behavior and compliance with Jesus' command to
leave the man express a universal truth: *Jesus' power and authority is
greater than Satan's.*

Reinforce this point by soliciting a contemporary example: *Who can share
a time you or someone you know saw Jesus' power triumph over evil?*

DEUTERONOMY 6:1-9

Verses 7–9 of this passage call for parental teaching that's persistent, spontaneous, informal, and responsive to teachable moments in the daily routine. First, pose an analytical question so they identify these characteristics of parental nurture: *How would you describe the kind of parental teaching called for in these verses?*

To fortify the point and encourage people to apply it, ask: *Who can give an example of parental Bible instruction that's been prompted by an unexpected occurrence or teachable moment?*

Ask for anecdotes only after you've already guided the group through the observation and interpretation phases of Bible study. God's truth—not personal experience—is the focal point of the discussion. The truth you're seeking to illustrate always deserves top billing. Yet slice-of-life stories solidify God's truth in learners' minds and jog their thinking about application. So be sure to move from understanding a Bible truth to illustrating how it can affect people's lives.

Charles Spurgeon, a prolific pastor of the nineteenth century, knew that Bible truths eclipse illustrations in importance. Yet he realized that folks are more likely to remember and to obey a truth that's illustrated. What he told aspiring preachers also pertains to classroom teachers and discussion facilitators: "Examples are more powerful than precepts."[2]

Step 4: Probe for Possibilities—The next step in the application process draws out realistic ways to respond to God's truth. In addition to soliciting anecdotes from the past picturing a precept in action, ask group members to imagine what application of the precept will look like. The ideas they present won't fit every participant, but when application ideas saturate their minds, the Holy Spirit has fuel to work with after the group disperses. This sort of probe creates a holy dissatisfaction with the status quo in people's lives.

Once again, let's look at examples from Matthew 4 and Deuteronomy 6.

MATTHEW 4:1-11

That Satan tempted Jesus three times, not just once, unveils the following insight: *In his attempts to derail God's purposes and defeat God's people, Satan is persistent.*

Here's how to probe for practical implications. *What difference should awareness of Satan's persistence make in our lives?*

An appropriate answer is that we should be just as relentless in our walk with God as Satan is in his attacks. A call to *our* persistence correctly identifies the truth's broad implication for God's people. But to abandon the principle at this point would abort the application process. Keep going until group members think in specific rather than general terms. Here's a way to follow up the first question:

> **Commentary**—The passage suggests that Christian living inevitably involves spiritual warfare. And as you pointed out, our persistence must match Satan's.
>
> **Question**—*How will persistence show in the life of a mature believer?* (You want them to identify outcomes such as prayer, Bible study, worship service attendance, a commitment to faith-strengthening fellowship, and consistent involvement in ministry.)

DEUTERONOMY 6:1–9

What follows is a conclusion couched in these verses: *Parents' spiritual training of children cannot be divorced from their own walk with God. Persistent and timely teaching of children stems from and depends on parents' love relationship with God, and their heartfelt knowledge of His word.*

Guiding the group to consider potential repercussions may require a series of life-related probes. Here's one approach:

- The precept identifies two parental responsibilities: nurturing a close relationship with the Lord, and nurturing kids in the faith. *How do parents sometimes focus on one responsibility at the exclusion of the other?*
- *To what extent is it possible to spend lots of energy on kids' spiritual development, yet neglect our daily walk with God?*
- *What obstacles do moms and dads face in keeping their hearts warm toward God and their minds steeped in God's Word?*
- Imagine that a married couple studies Deuteronomy 6:1–9 together. They conclude that their love for God is lukewarm. They often expose

their kids to God's Word, but their own intake amounts to an 800-calorie-per-day diet. Now they're determined to change. *What type of things can they do to align their lives with the commands in this passage?*

Step 5: Learn Your Limitations—I previously defined "teaching for application" as *the process of guiding a group to identify follow-through possibilities.* You set the stage for lesson response, but your group members are the performers. They're responsible before God to reform their relationships, reverse sinful patterns, and meet needs around them as dictated by the Bible passage.

You can reserve group time to discuss a truth's implications. You can testify to the power of the passage in your own life. You can help people picture the difference a precept would make if they incorporated it in their daily routines. You can ask them for anecdotes that disclose the benefits of obeying and the consequences of neglecting God's Word. You can probe for possible responses that fit the needs and maturity levels of participants. *But you cannot apply God's Word for anyone but yourself!* A learner's heart is either fertile soil that welcomes the seed of Scripture, or rocky ground too callous for the seed to penetrate.

There's a logical reaction to realizing your limitations: *pray for your group members.* When you intercede for them, you're acknowledging dependence on the Holy Spirit. You're admitting that transferring truth from the head to the heart is a divine rather than a human endeavor. You're asking God to accomplish what no amount of teaching excellence can: to prick their consciences, to alter their attitudes, and to bend their wills in the direction of biblical standards. This reliance on God for life change in learners reminds me of something W. E. Sangster said: "God's work, apart from prayer, produces *clever ineffectiveness.*"[3]

Make the following prayer your own. The wording implies that leading a group is a mysterious, cooperative effort between human and divine agents of change.

A PRAYER FOR APPLICATION

Father, I'm responsible to strive for life change in my teaching. During both the preparation and presentation phases of each Bible lesson, there are things I can do to encourage application. Yet I'm aware of my limitations.

Only you can cause a person to loathe sin. Only you can instill joy in a heart that's hurting. Only you can reconcile family members who haven't spoken to each other in years. Only you can mold a person's will until he wants to obey your Word. So if life change is going to occur among the members of my group, you must soften their hearts. You must encourage attitudes, thoughts, and behaviors in line with the lesson. I'll do my part and commit group time to probe possible applications. But the last thing I want to be, Lord, is cleverly ineffective. In the name of One who prayed for the people He taught, Amen.

On the preceding pages you've seen how to formulate observation, interpretation, and application questions. But you may be wondering how the various kinds of questions work together within a single Bible lesson. Is there a step-by-step approach to structuring a sound discussion plan? What kind of format encourages progression from *knowledge* to *comprehension* to *changed lives?* Let's proceed to the next chapter and find out.

CHAPTER SIX

Organizing Your Bible Discussion

JOE ARRIVED EARLY for the senior high Bible study that he leads. He pinned a large sheet of newsprint to the wall and printed the following incomplete sentence along the top:

Temptation is_____.

As teens arrived, he gave them a magic marker and instructed everyone to complete the sentence. To launch the study on Matthew 4:1–11, titled "Winning at Spiritual Warfare," he referred to the newsprint and read aloud several contributions:

- *When I want a second helping of ice cream pie.*
- *When my dad jumps on my back for no good reason, and I feel like telling him off.*
- *A girl wearing skin-tight jeans and a braless halter top.*
- *A voice inside me, coaxing me to do something I know is wrong.*
- *Somebody else's test paper when I need a good grade to pass the course.*
- *Hard to resist!*

Then Joe used the following remarks to provide transition into the Bible study: "Experiencing temptation is not sin. Jesus was tempted, yet He was sinless. The crunch is, how do we respond to it? As we examine Matthew 4:1–11, we'll wrestle with these questions: When temptation strikes, what difference should our faith make? What advantages does a Christian have in responding to the lure of the world? What strategy for resisting temptation did Jesus model for us? Applying today's lesson won't wipe out temptations . . . but it can keep us from yielding to them."

Why did Joe launch his lesson in this manner? Why didn't he jump right into the Bible passage?

Joe displayed a keen sensitivity to lesson organization. He designed an opening activity that prepared kids for the Bible study, that revealed the significance of the passage to be investigated. Joe knows how to structure the group time for maximum impact.

Whether you teach a Sunday school class or lead a small group study, you'll enhance your effectiveness by organizing your material logically. On the following pages, you'll identify the basic parts of a sound lesson plan and examine the line of reasoning behind the pattern. You'll also discover a format that gets group members into God's Book—and gets God's Book into group members. And you'll see how the various types of discussion questions fit into the structure.

Most publishers of church curriculum materials or leader's guides for groups follow a similar organizational pattern. Their terminology for the various parts of the lesson differs, but their Bible study procedure—the instructional process that's outlined in a lesson—follows the same educationally-sound structure. What follows is my own simple version that can serve as a framework for your group sessions: **Approach the Word, Absorb the Word, and Apply the Word.**

APPROACH THE WORD

Folks come to your study group operating at varying wavelengths. Though they've chosen to attend, it isn't safe to assume their minds are on the upcoming Bible lesson. Sally feels uptight about a recent argument with her daughter. Bill is dragging from lack of sleep. Jane's trying to remember if she turned off the burner under the pot of beans. Chad keeps replaying Friday night's football game, nagging himself over that costly fumble. Nicole won't admit it, but she's looking around to see if Ronnie has arrived. He seems interested in her, but she's wondering if he'll ever get around to asking her out.

Numerous "inner factors," usually unknown to the leader, operate within group members. Since other people or personal circumstances claim their attention, it's difficult for them to jump right into a Bible lesson. So in view of human nature, a wise teacher or discussion facilitator plans to "Approach the Word" before investigating it.

What should this opening lesson segment accomplish? Whatever you do or say should lead group members into thinking about the topic or lesson theme. Begin with a life-related activity that makes people leave their train of thought and focus instead on the subject of the lesson. Rather than *assume* people's interest in the Bible passage, you *earn* it.

Grab group members' attention by raising a question, referring to a problem, or introducing an issue that's relevant to them and which the Bible passage will address. Your "Approach the Word" segment should tap into some felt need within learners and give them a reason for paying attention. An approach activity is brief, usually three to five minutes. It should increase anticipation for the study and lead smoothly and logically into the Bible passage for the day.

You can select from a wide range of methods: questions, illustrations, word association, object lessons, thought-provoking quotations, humor, sentence completions. Vary your approach from week to week, making sure it accomplishes its purpose. Then develop a transition that leads logically into the Bible passage.

Here's an example of an "Approach the Word" segment.

Pam launched her ladies' Bible study by displaying a thermometer. She explained that one's body temperature is a vital sign of physical health. If a young child acts cranky and mopes around, we pop a thermometer into his mouth. If his temp is elevated, it's a sign of trouble within the body. Some sort of infection has set in. Then Pam posed a question: *"How is our tongue like a thermometer?"*

The respondents saw the point of the analogy. They pointed out that words are an indicator of our spiritual health.

Next, Pam offered the following transition into the Bible study: *"I've titled today's Bible study 'The Thermometer of the Heart'. In Luke 6:45, Jesus said that a person's mouth 'speaks from that which fills his heart.' Just as body temperature is a vital sign of physical health, our speech patterns are a vital sign of our spiritual health. What practical guidelines does God offer as a reference point for evaluating our daily conversations? How can we use the tongue to help others instead of harm them? Let's turn to a verse that addresses these questions: Ephesians 4:29. What we discover may expose an infection needing an immediate antidote. Or it may inoculate us against diseases that typically afflict the human heart."*

Whether you call it an *introduction*, a *hook*, a *focusing activity*, a *lesson launch*, or an *approach*, the opening segment whets your group's appetite for God's Word.

Absorb the Word

To *absorb* means "to take in and make a part of one's being." That's precisely your goal during a Bible study! You want group members' exposure to Scripture to result in their assimilation of it. That's why you devote a majority of your meeting time to direct investigation of a Bible passage. Group Bible discussion is a natural extension of the introduction. Group members' attention shifts to God's perspectives on the issue, problem, or question you raised during the "Approach the Word" segment.

During this "Absorb the Word" phase of the lesson, participants experience the *observation* and *interpretation* steps of Bible study (see Chapters 3 and 4). You familiarize people with what the passage says and guide them to timeless truths implied or illustrated by the content. For youth and adult groups, you employ teaching techniques that propel learners into the biblical text to discover truth for themselves.

Crack open curriculum manuals or leader's guides offered by Christian publishers and you'll uncover a variety of terminology for this investigative phase of the lesson: **Lesson Development; Explore; Discover;** and **Bible Learning**, to name a few. No matter how you label it, *this section outlines a step-by-step strategy for covering lesson content.*

As a discussion leader, you'll prompt participants' investigation of Scripture with a combination of observation and interpretation questions. To develop this "Absorb the Word" segment of your discussion plan, here's how to proceed:

> **Step 1—** Identify the important facts and truths you need to cover during the group meeting. (Chapters 3 and 4 provide study methods for finding the facts and precepts, plus guidelines for selecting which passage elements to cover.)

Step 2— *Write discussion questions that will enable group members to find the facts and articulate the precepts.* (To polish wording of your probes, consult Chapter 7: "Guidelines for Effective Questions.")

Step 3— *Jot down your own answer to each question you formulate.* (Recording what you perceive to be correct or ideal responses has two advantages. First, you'll be ready to supplement group members' contributions with insights of your own. That's especially helpful when questions have two or more possible answers. Second, your detailed notes will come in handy the next time you teach this passage. You'll save hours because you won't have to take the time to reexamine the text for the purpose of looking up answers long forgotten.)

Step 4— *Determine the lecture segments needed to fill out your teaching plan. Within the series of questions, insert skeletal lecture notes on historical background, word studies, controversial doctrines, and illustrations.* (The "Absorb the Word" segment will consist of everything you plan *to ask* and *to say*, arranged in the order in which you envision it occurring. It's a description of the sequential *procedure* for group examination of the Bible passage.)

Remember Pam's lesson on "The Thermometer of the Heart"? The entire "Absorb the Word" segment of her discussion plan focused on Ephesians 4:29:

> Let no unwholesome word proceed from your mouth, but only such a word as is good for edification, according to the need of the moment, that it may give grace to those who hear.

Pam presented a couple of minutes of contextual information, showing how the verse fits into the flow of the epistle. To enhance people's understanding of Paul's intent, she shared brief word studies on the terms "unwholesome," "edification," and "grace." Then she instructed the ladies to work with a partner and jot down answers to this question: *What guidelines for daily conversation can you glean from this verse?* Ten minutes later, participants reported on their findings. Together, group members polished the wording of the various contributions and put the guidelines in the form of four questions for self-evaluation:

1. Are any of my words impure and unwholesome?
2. Do my words build up or tear down other people?
3. Is the motive behind my words to meet the needs of others?
4. Do my words "give grace" to those who hear, or about whom I'm talking?

Pam's mini-lecture on the verse's context, her word studies, the pairs' development of conversation guidelines, and the process of restating those guidelines in the form of questions were the components of her "Absorb the Word" section. The ladies observed what Paul said, then interpreted it by formulating timeless principles pertaining to the tongue.

For an additional example of an "Absorb the Word" section of a discussion plan, see the lesson I've included at the end of this chapter.

APPLY THE WORD

As emphasized in Chapter 5, "Preparing Application Questions," you'll devote part of your group meeting to the Bible's *significance* for participants. Together, you'll probe the practical implications of material that you observe and interpret. By planning an "Apply the Word" segment, you're acknowledging that behavior change—not knowledge—is the ultimate purpose of Bible study. I defined this application phase of your session as:

The joint effort to identify attitude and lifestyle changes that spring logically from Bible truths. Together, you ponder how God's truth should affect participants' priorities, emotions, decisions, and relationships.

Why insert a separate section on application into your discussion plan? Because if you don't plan to discuss a lesson's life implications, other group activities or coverage of content will consume all the meeting time. A section labeled "Apply the Word" serves as a visible reminder to emphasize it. Also, many learners don't discern potential responses to God's truth on their own. They need group interaction to stimulate their thinking. The questions and anecdotes they hear help them connect the content to their own circumstances.

As in the "Absorb the Word" lesson phase, crafting this section requires *listing the questions you plan to ask, in succession.* The "Ask for Anecdotes" and "Probe for Possibilities" sections of Chapter 5 illustrate two types of inquiries that spur thinking about lesson follow-through. How long you spend in the "Apply the Word" part of the lesson depends on the nature of your Bible passage; the needs or background of group members; and the total amount of time you have for the group meeting. In most cases, between 20 and 30 percent of your total group time should be spent on this "Apply the Word" segment.

To illustrate an "Apply the Word" segment, here's what Pam asked in her lesson on Ephesians 4:29:

- **In what kind of situations are we prone to use "unwholesome" speech?**
- **What are examples of words that build up others spiritually? That unnecessarily tear them down?**
- **Who can share a time when you felt edified as a result of someone's words?**
- **What character traits must we develop before we can meet needs with our words?**
- **Often we sin with words in response to people who hurt us with their tongue. For instance, we're prone to retaliate when another person gossips about us. How does Paul's call for "gracious" speech fit into such a scenario?**

To conclude her "Apply the Word" segment, Pam asked the following rhetorical questions and followed them with a couple of minutes of silent prayer.

- **What relationships came to mind as we identified the speech guidelines in Ephesians 4:29?**
- **Why did God's Spirit bring those people to mind? Is there someone you've sinned against, from whom you need to seek forgiveness? Or did you think of someone who needs the encouragement your words can offer?**
- **Look over the four conversation guidelines we developed. To be in conformity to God's Word, which guideline do you most need to work on in your daily conversations?**

SWITCH THE SEQUENCE

If you glanced at Pam's written discussion plan, you'd see her lecture notes and the development of conversation guidelines under a section labeled "Absorb the Word." Then you'd see her series of life-related questions in a separate lesson segment marked "Apply the Word." Often that's a natural approach to organizing your questions: List the observation and interpretation assignments, then conclude with all the application inquiries. In such a format, all life-related questions are set apart from the Bible discovery segment.

But sometimes it's more effective to employ a few application questions within the "Absorb the Word" part of the lesson. Rather than reserve all life-related inquiries for a separate segment, follow the observation-interpretation-application pattern on a given truth or verse. Then move to a different passage element and start over again with either observation or interpretation exercises.

Here's a list of questions from the "Absorb The Word" segment of Joe's discussion plan on Matthew 4:1–11. Notice how he mixes the various kinds of questions during the passage investigation:

Observation—What were the three temptations that Satan threw at Jesus?

Observation—What did Jesus' response to the three temptations have in common?

Application—Who can illustrate how the power of God's Word helps a person defend against temptation?

Interpretation—Satan tempted Jesus three times, not just once. What does that fact tell us about Satan?

Application—What difference should it make in our lives to know that Satan is persistent?

Application—If we're persistent in our efforts to follow Christ and resist temptation, how will it show in our schedules?

Switching the sequence of questions does not erase the need for a separate "Apply the Word" lesson segment. It's still a top-shelf priority to reserve time for personal reflection on the passage as a whole. Mixing in a few application questions simply means you probe practical implications of points *as they crop up*, rather than reserving all application questions for the concluding segment.

In this chapter, you've learned how to organize a discussion plan for leading a Bible study. What follows is a start-to-finish discussion plan that illustrates the format I've described. After examining this sample, reserve a spot in your schedule to read Chapter 7. There you'll learn more about developing questions that are Biblically and educationally sound.

DISCUSSION PLAN FOR PHILIPPIANS 1:1–11
HOW CHRISTIAN FELLOWSHIP SHOWS

Paul and Timothy, bond-servants of Christ Jesus, to all the saints in Christ Jesus who are in Philippi, including the overseers and deacons: Grace to you and peace from God our Father and the Lord Jesus Christ.

I thank my God in all my remembrance of you, always offering prayer with joy in my every prayer for you all, in view of your participation in the gospel from the first day until now. For I am confident of this very thing, that He who began a good work in you will perfect it until the day of Christ Jesus. For it is only right for me to feel this way about you all, because I have you in my heart, since both in my imprisonment and in the defense and con-firmation of the gospel, you all are partakers of grace with me. For God is my witness, how I long for you all with the affection of Christ Jesus. And this I pray, that your love may abound still more and more in real knowledge and all discernment, so that you may approve the things that are excellent, in order to be sincere and blameless until the day of Christ; having been filled with the fruit of righteousness which comes through Jesus Christ, to the glory and praise of God.

Theme Statement—Philippians 1:1–11 offers timeless expressions of Christian fellowship.

APPROACH THE WORD

What do you associate with the word "fellowship?" What comes to your mind when you see or hear this word?

Transition into Bible Lesson—We have told what we associate with the word "fellowship," and we've shared some of our experiences. But it is even more important to know what God associates with the word. From God's perspective, what does genuine fellowship look like? What type of things does He want us to experience in our relationships with other Christians? We can find answers to those questions in Paul's introduction to the book of Philippians. Let's turn to Philippians 1:1–11 and find time-less expressions of fellowship that should describe our relationships, too.

ABSORB THE WORD

LECTURE—Give 2-3 minutes of background to the letter of Philippians. Review how the Philippian church was founded, using information in Acts 16, and how close relationships started between Paul's team and people like Lydia and the jailor. Mention that Paul wrote the Philippian letter from prison in Rome, primarily to thank them for their prayers and for a finan-cial contribution they made to his ministry (see Phil. 4:14–16). Refer to verse 5 of Chapter 1, where Paul mentioned "your participation in the gospel." The word "participation" is the word "koinonia," which is also translated "fellowship." (Next, ask each group member to read 1:1–11 silently from his own Bible.)

DISCUSSION—

Observation—What word did Paul use to describe himself and Timothy? (bondservant, v.1)

Interpretation—What does that word tell us about their attitude, and their purpose in life? (It means they considered themselves the property of Christ. They were at His complete disposal, fully committed to Him. Their purpose was to serve Him by telling others about Him.)

Interpretation—How would you describe the mood, or emotional atmosphere, of verses 3–11? (warm, friendly, positive, thankful)

Observation—What words/phrases from this passage show that Paul and the Philippians enjoyed a close relationship?

v.3—"I thank God in all my remembrance of you"
v.4—"offering prayer . . . for you all"
v.5—"your participation in the gospel"

v.7—"to feel this way about you"
v.7—"I have you in my heart"
v.8—"I long for you all with the affection of Christ"
v.9—"I pray . . . [for you]"

Interpretation—(At this point in the study, give a longer "interpretation" assignment. Now that they are familiar with the passage, help them to identify principles about "fellowship," or see timeless expressions of fellowship illustrated in those verses.)

Divide into pairs. Take 5-6 minutes to work together and write down answers to this question: What timeless expressions of fellowship did Paul and the Philippians model for us? (How did their fellowship show?) After 5-6 minutes, reconvene and ask volunteers to share answers with the whole class. Supplement their answers as needed from the following list:

* wrote letters when physically separated, to offer encouragement and counsel (Paul wrote them!)
* exercised ministry of intercessory prayer for one another (vv. 4, 9–11)
* gave to meet material needs (Philippians gave $ to Paul - implied vs. 5)
* openly expressed affection, instead of taking positive feelings we have for granted (tell others we love them - vv. 7–8)
* Christian fellowship was rooted in a deep commitment to Jesus Christ (implied in vs. 1, "bondservant of Christ")
* shared experiences/time together crucial to developing fellowship (v.3 "my remembrance of you" referred to events recorded in Acts 16.)

Illustration—Paul openly expressed his affection to the Philippians by writing a letter, and telling them he loved them. A Christian man expressed his love for a hurting couple by writing the following poem. Like Paul, he found a concrete way to express affection. It is titled, "I'm Wearing Your Skin."

When your mind ponders what might have been,
And despondently wonders why you can't win,
I also reflect on recent days
 And feel the effect of insensitive ways.

When you laugh, I do.
When you weep, me too!
Through thick and thin,
I'm wearing your skin.
When you feel insecure about a plan's revision,
And wish you had fewer times of decision;
Then my situation becomes unglued,
And my relationship to pain is renewed.
Whatever you feel, to some degree,
Works its way into me.
Through your ups and downs, I'm spiritual kin—
I'm wearing your skin!

APPLY THE WORD

Who can share about a time you experienced one of the expressions of fellowship modeled by Paul and the Philippians?

(Personal Reflection)—How common are these expressions of fellowship among Christians you know? To what extent are you experiencing the type of fellowship illustrated in Phil.1:1–11?

LECTURE—Too often we wait for other believers to take initiative to reach out to us. We think only of receiving acts of friendship and fellowship. But maybe God wants us to take the initiative and start building closer relationships with Christians we know.

Application Project—Think about the ways fellowship showed between Paul and the Philippians. Decide on one thing you can do this week to express concern for, or initiate fellowship with, an individual or a group of believers. (Write someone an encouraging letter? Help a struggling believer out financially? Begin a ministry of intercession for a brother in need? Etc.)

Close in a time of silent prayer, asking God to help you take the initiative with someone.

CHAPTER SEVEN

GUIDELINES FOR EFFECTIVE QUESTIONS

W HEN IT COMES to taking potshots at the English language, these two usually hit the bull's-eye. When someone writes the book on ambiguity, their names will appear in ALL CAPS and **bold-faced print**. When it comes to the championship of muddled conversation, they're in the final round of the playoffs. Their names? Jerry Coleman, baseball announcer for the San Diego Padres, and Yogi Berra, Hall of Fame catcher and former New York Yankees manager.

Jerry has made the following remarks over the air:

"Rick Rolkers is throwing up in the bullpen."

"They throw Winfield out at second base and he's safe."

"Winfield goes back to the wall. He hits his head on the wall and it rolls off! It's rolling all the way back to second base! This is a terrible thing for the Padres!"

"McCovey swings and misses, and it's fouled back."

Berra has provided stiff competition for Coleman. On a hot day in St. Petersburg, Florida, a spring training observer once told Yogi, "Good afternoon, Mr. Berra. My, you look mighty cool today." "Thank you, ma'am," Yogi replied. "You don't look so hot yourself."

Other ingenious observations attributed to Berra include:

"We lost because we made too many wrong mistakes."

"A nickel ain't worth a dime anymore."

"Baseball is 90 percent mental. The other half is physical."

"You got to be careful if you don't know where you're going, because you might not get there."

Confusing commentary may be a genetic endowment. Dale Berra followed in his dad's footsteps as a conversationalist as well as a professional baseball player. Talking to a reporter about his famous dad, Dale said, "The similarities between me and my father are different."[1]

When it comes to entertaining a group, notorious quipsters like Coleman and Berra hit a homer every time. But when it comes to leading effective discussions, they wouldn't even make it to first base. We may experience rib-tickling delight from a sampling of fuzzy communication, but when leading a Bible study, precise language is a must. Compete with Coleman or the Berras and group members will stay away in droves. Effective group leaders are *word carpenters*. What learners think you're saying must match what you intended to say.

That's why this chapter zeroes in on wording questions correctly. In past chapters, you've learned a lot about the types of questions to ask and when to ask them. But to apply all that knowledge *about* discussion you need to be able to hammer out sound questions. What you learn in this chapter will prepare you to adapt questions provided in curriculum materials or to come up with your own fog-lifting questions for Bible study discussions.

WINNING AT WARFARE

To illustrate question guidelines throughout this chapter, I'll continue with the record of Jesus' wilderness temptations prior to the launch of His public ministry. Take a moment to skim the narrative.

MATTHEW 4:1-11

Then Jesus was led up by the Spirit into the wilderness to be tempted by the devil. And after He had fasted forty days and forty nights, He then became hungry. And the tempter came and said to Him, "If You are the Son of God, command that these stones become bread." But He answered and said, "It is written, 'MAN SHALL NOT LIVE ON BREAD ALONE, BUT

ON EVERY WORD THAT PROCEEDS OUT OF THE MOUTH OF GOD.'"
Then the devil took Him into the holy city; and he had Him stand on the
pinnacle of the temple, and said to Him, "If You are the Son of God
throw Yourself down; for it is written, 'HE WILL GIVE HIS ANGELS
CHARGE CONCERNING YOU' and 'ON THEIR HANDS THEY WILL
BEAR YOU UP, LEST YOU STRIKE YOUR FOOT AGAINST A STONE.'"
Jesus said to him, "On the other hand, it is written, 'YOU SHALL NOT
PUT THE LORD YOUR GOD TO THE TEST.'" Again, the devil took Him
to a very high mountain, and showed Him all the kingdoms of the world,
and their glory; and he said to Him, "All these things will I give You, if
You fall down and worship me." Then Jesus said to him, "Begone, Satan!
For it is written, 'YOU SHALL WORSHIP THE LORD YOUR GOD, AND
SERVE HIM ONLY.'" Then the devil left Him; and behold, angels came
and began to minister to Him.

Here's the main theme I gleaned from the passage: *By examining Jesus'
bout with Satan, we gain insights to help us experience victory in spiritual
warfare.* In a typical Bible study on these verses, I'd emphasize two primary truths: (1) *Satan's temptation of Jesus reveals characteristics and strategies that still distinguish his warfare against Christians.* (2) *Jesus' method of
resisting Satan shows how we can rebuff him. Hiding God's Word in our
hearts provides the strength and perspective necessary for successful spiritual
warfare.*

Now that you're familiar with the narrative and the primary truths in
the passage, we can zero in on the characteristics of effective questions.

FEATURES OF EFFECTIVE QUESTIONS

The verb "cast" means "to toss, to put forth." As a small group facilitator or
Sunday school teacher, that's what you do with questions. You cast
inquiries at group members and hope your words lead to thought and discovery. I'll employ the term CAST as an acronym for four features of well-
worded Bible study questions. They're Clear, Accurate, Sensitive, and
Thought-provoking. A skillful discussion leader caters to clarity, aims for
accuracy, strives for sensitivity, and incites the intellect.

CATER TO CLARITY

The following quotation was spotted on a graffiti wall at St. John's University in Minnesota:

> Jesus said to them, "Who do you say that I am?"
> And they replied, "You are the eschatological manifestation of the ground of our being, the kerygma in which we find the ultimate meaning of our interpersonal relationships."
> And Jesus said, "*What?*"[2]

This imaginary dialogue reminds me of Jesus' habit of putting the bread of life on the lowest shelf, where anyone could reach it. Neither high-falutin' vocabulary nor abstract oratory impresses Him—or your group members! Plain, easy-to-grasp English is the first feature of questions that pry open the human mind.

Put yourself in the Reeboks of your group members. Will they understand the vocabulary in your questions? Does your wording presume too much biblical or theological knowledge on their part? Can you insert a shorter word for the long one? C.S. Lewis' advice to writers also merits the attention of Bible study leaders. What he told an aspiring author is conveyed in these words: "If it's possible to be misunderstood, you will be!"[3] Inspect questions for ambiguity. Recite questions aloud. Test them on your spouse or a friend to see if the intent is clear. And be on the lookout for the following foes of clarity.

"What About" Questions—One type of question that always drops a dark veil over group members' thinking begins with the words, "*What about . . .?*" It's a common way to launch a question in casual conversations. (*What about the prayer request you mentioned last week?*) But never allow "what about" to trespass into the domain of Bible study questions.

Suppose I ask, *What about the fact that Satan quoted Scripture in his confrontation with Jesus?* Your participants' logical reaction? A shrug of their shoulders. And a question of their own. "Well, *what about it?*"

Whoever poses that particular question may be exploring something important, but just not addressing it properly. Perhaps the leader wants to discuss what Satan's use of Scripture implies about him. If that's the case, stimulate thinking by asking: *What's significant about Satan's use of Scripture?*

Run-Together Questions—Rein in the impulse to fling back-to-back questions at the group without waiting for a reply to the first one. *One question at a time!* I can't think of a valid exception to that rule. A review of research on questions delivered in college classrooms echoes this point. The authors concluded, "A major source of ambiguity is the use of run-on questions. In this case two or more questions are asked in an uninterrupted series and the students do not know which question the teacher wants answered."[4]

These Bible questions will encourage learner participation . . . *if* you don't pronounce them in the same breath: *Notice the preceding events in Matthew 3. At what point in Jesus' earthly ministry did this temptation episode occur? Why did Satan pick this particular time to launch his attack?*

Long-Winded Questions—Another nemesis of clarity is the long-winded question. A good discussion facilitator trims the fat off an overweight question until it is lean enough to appear in a Slim-Fast commercial. Research on teaching has identified factors that enhance or hamper learner participation in the classroom. A skill essential to eliciting discussion is

> Wording the query appropriately. . . . Experienced instructors . . . keep their queries short and simple. There is an inverse relationship between the number of words in an instructor's probe and the length of subsequent student comments. If students must work to decipher your question, they are less likely to respond to it.[5]

Which question gets your vote for less complicated?

Looking at the devil in action tempting Jesus in the wilderness, what specific qualities and strategies of spiritual warfare that he will also use against us does he demonstrate?

Or . . .

What do we learn about Satan from this incident?

Let's take a cue from Jesus. His questions were crisp and terse—often disturbing, but understandable. The pages of the Gospels are stitched together with examples of His compelling probes. The following examples spurred thought among those listening to Jesus:

"Who do people say that the Son of Man is?" (Matthew 16:13).

"Why do you discuss the fact that you have no bread?" (Mark 8:17).

"Why are you anxious about clothing?" (Matthew 6:28).

"How can you, being evil, speak what is good?" (Matthew 12:34).

"Why do you call Me, 'Lord, Lord,' and do not do what I say?" (Luke 6:46).

"How is it that the scribes say that the Christ is the son of David?" (Mark 12:35).

"Will you lay down your life for Me?" (John 13:38).

A sure-fire way to prune the clutter from questions is to precede them with introductory remarks. Facts we stuff within the probe itself are more easily assimilated by learners when we put them in statements. The following question is too long and cumbersome:

> In light of the way Jesus responded to each of the three temptations by saying, "It is written," what principle about succeeding in spiritual warfare can we learn from Him?

Instead, put the necessary facts into statements. Then use a shorter, easier-to-grasp question:

> Look again at the verses recording Jesus' response to each temptation. On each occasion He employed the phrase, "It is written." What insight about handling temptation did He model for us?

There's yet another way to cover facts that are foundational to questions. Set the stage for interpretation by posing an observation question.

> *Observation*—What did Jesus' responses to the three temptations have in common?

Then move on to the next step . . .

> *Interpretation*—What insight about handling temptation did He model for us?

Questions Dependent on Particular Translations—A question that relies on a particular Bible translation may cause ambiguity. Perhaps you do your mining in the *New American Standard Bible*, but group members excavate their inspired nuggets from the *New International Version* or the *New King James Version* or *The Living Bible*. When you base an inquiry on a particular word or phrase, check it out in the versions preferred by participants.

I'll never forget the time I relied on my *New American Standard* translation to form a question for a group of new believers. We were parked in Ephesians 4 during a twelve-week ride through the epistle. I directed people to verses 11–12 and told them Paul used the term "equip" to describe the basic job of church leaders. Then I asked, "*What does the word 'equip' imply about the work of the church?*" The college student toting an NIV frowned. A King James advocate furrowed his eyebrows. The couple holding a paraphrase kept skimming Ephesians 4 looking for a verse containing "equip." They didn't pick up on synonyms such as "prepare" (NIV) or "perfect" (KJV).

In Matthew 4:1–11, the NASB refers to the "glory" of the kingdoms offered to Jesus (vs. 8). The NIV prefers the term "splendor." Where the NASB has angels "ministering" to Jesus (vs. 11), they "attended" Him in the NIV. These particular word differences probably won't confuse anyone. But ignoring subtle variations among translations will eventually embarrass you.

As important as clear wording is, it means little without the next characteristic of effective questions. After all, a question can be *clearly erroneous* in its approach to Scripture.

Aim for Accuracy

Whether you teach a teen Sunday school class, lead a Bible study in a women's prison, or facilitate a discussion with mature adults, *your cardinal goal is accuracy.* The same holds true whether you circle metal chairs in the corner of a gymnasium, sit on the plush carpet of a multi-million dollar educational facility, or huddle around the fireplace in your den. Whether you're going through a Bible book verse-by-verse or exploring a contemporary issue through the lens of Scripture. Whether you use a wide assortment of creative methods or stick to plain old question-and-answer.

When it comes to Bible study, what group members conclude about a passage should match its God-intended meaning. I've encountered four adversaries to accuracy that crop up in the wording of discussion questions. Leaders risk inaccuracy when their queries:

- *Foster speculation about the text*
- *Encourage exploration of irrelevant material*
- *Shift the focus of authority from God's Word to participants' opinions*
- *Confuse the meaning of Bible content with its significance for our lives*

Speculative Questions—As a teacher or discussion facilitator, you're a guide who leads others on safaris into the biblical text. But when a speculative question slips into the group interaction, you may get lost in a maze of misinterpretation or meaningless mumbo-jumbo. A speculative question seeks information not disclosed in the Bible passage and tries to satisfy curiosity about a fact God figured we didn't need to know. It also promotes conjecture about the Bible rather than investigation and analysis of it.

You won't hear me ask the following questions during a study of Matthew 4:1–11. No matter how long participants pore over the verses, they won't find an answer.

> Jesus' baptism at the hands of John the Baptist preceded this temptation narrative (Matthew 3:13–17). How much time do you think elapsed between the baptism and His excursion into the wilderness?
> If Jesus had listened to Satan and jumped off the pinnacle of the temple, what do you think would have happened?
> The devil promised Jesus all the kingdoms of the world (vv. 8–9). Would that promise have been fulfilled if Jesus had worshiped Satan?
> When the devil left, angels came and ministered to Jesus (v. 11). How do you think the angels ministered to Him in this situation?

Irrelevant Questions—Ever heard Bible study questions that "majored on the minors?" Queries that dissected a word, phrase, or name in a verse without consideration of its larger context or sought definitions or details you couldn't connect to the theme of the lesson? Then you were victimized by *irrelevant questions*.

Aiming for accuracy in a discussion isn't only a matter of avoiding speculation and outright error. It's also sticking to the overarching theme of a text, covering just those facts and truths that develop your subject slant. When less significant passage data steal the spotlight, discussion becomes a game of "trivial pursuit."

Allow me to return to the theme of Matthew 4:1–11: *By examining Jesus' bout with Satan, we gain insights to help us experience victory in spiritual warfare.* Matthew weaves two threads of thought through the fabric of these verses. He illustrates battle strategies and characteristics of Satan, our archenemy. And through the example of Jesus, he shows us the value of Scripture as a defense against temptation. All study questions I toss at the group should reinforce the primary theme and lead to discovery, analysis, and application of the two more specific subject slants. With that in mind, you'll understand my contempt for the following questions. These inquiries examine passage elements in piecemeal fashion, rather than connecting details to the unifying lesson theme.

> According to verse 2, Jesus fasted prior to the clash with Satan. What is the value of fasting in the life of a Christian? Why don't more Christians fast?
>
> Jesus fasted for forty days and forty nights. What are some other occasions in the Bible when a forty-day time period was significant?
>
> Matthew labeled Jerusalem a "holy" city (v. 5). Why did He use that particular adjective?

Questions That Usurp Biblical Authority—Another way to encourage an inaccurate interpretation of a Bible passage is to transfer the authority from God's Word to the group members. Now I know you'd never do such a thing intentionally, but it often happens when a group leader is inexperienced or poorly prepared.

In an article in *Christianity Today,* Walt Russell published his diagnosis of this discussion-group disease. He labeled it *relativism.* He believes this infection has reached epidemic proportions in Sunday school classes and home Bible study gatherings. And every time a leader asks, "*What do you think this verse means?*" the virus spreads. According to Russell, when you pose this question,

The focus for determining meaning is now on the interpreter. The reader allegedly "creates meaning." Applied to Bible study, interpretation becomes not discovering the absolute truth of God's Word, but winning others to what the text "means to us" because our system for explaining it is the most internally coherent and satisfying . . . at least until a more . . . satisfying interpretation comes along.[6]

What steps can we take to safeguard biblical authority during our lessons? We can reserve another hour in our schedules for lesson preparation. Establish the historical context of a passage and work harder to discern the author's original intent. Consult Bible study resources to check the accuracy of our own conclusions. Take time with the group to absorb the facts of the passage before jumping to interpretation. Ask that every participant devote a half-hour to the Bible segment before the group meets. And we can ban language such as "*What does it mean to you?*"

Chapters 3–5 of this book explain the *observation-interpretation-application* stages of Bible study. Make it a top priority to grasp and apply that material. The recommendations there provide a sturdy foundation for the questioning guidelines in this chapter. When you have a handle on those chapters, you'll be well on your way to avoiding inappropriate questions.

Questions that Confuse "Meaning" and "Significance"—Confusing the meaning of a Bible verse with its application is a similar threat to accuracy. Well-intentioned leaders often use the "*What does this verse mean to you?*" question. This cliché often signals the beginning of the interpretation phase of a Bible study. The fact that the wording shifts authority from the Bible text to the participant is only one of its weaknesses. The question also mistakes a text's *meaning* for its *significance*.

As explained in Chapter 4, interpretation questions steer learners *into the Bible passage* for analysis and synthesis of facts. Tagging the "*mean-to-you?*" phrase onto the end of a question has the opposite effect. The "*mean-to-you?*" wording gives people a green light to look inside themselves, to dredge up past experiences, to recite somebody's opinion they've come across—everything but investigate the verse itself. *Meaning* always originates in the text. *Significance* (or application) describes a relationship between the text and a life situation. What a truth "means to me" is actually its implications for my attitudes and behavior. A text's *meaning* never changes, but its *significance* to me and to others is fluid and flexible.

Once again, let's look at Matthew 4:1–11. Don't launch a lesson on this passage, skim the narrative, then begin serious exploration with " *What does this episode mean to you?*" Instead, guide people into those verses and pepper your interpretation phase with questions of this sort:

What do Satan's actions and words tell us about him?

What tactics or warfare strategies does Satan demonstrate in His temptations of Jesus?

What does Jesus model for us about handling temptation?

Look closely at the Old Testament verses Jesus quoted. What is the relationship between the content of those verses and the nature or slant of the temptations?

Now that you know how to formulate questions to achieve clarity and accuracy, you're ready for the next guideline.

STRIVE FOR SENSITIVITY

When is a question *sensitive?* When you make personal responses voluntary. And when you're realistic about participants' ability to answer.

Compulsory Personal Questions—Sure, you want group members to reinforce truths with anecdotes. You want them to reveal needs exposed by God's Word so you can pray specifically for one another. In Chapter 2, we saw that *transparency* is a vital sign of a healthy group. In Chapter 5, we emphasized that soliciting illustrations can enhance a lesson's practicality. Go ahead and ask for examples of someone's applying a truth, or the consequences of neglecting it. Just don't drop a personal question in the lap of an unsuspecting learner.

What happens when you insist on an intimate disclosure? The person you finger may hotfoot it home and never return.

Let's assume your group is responding to this question on Matthew 4:1–11: *What does the incident teach us about Satan?* Marge blurts out, "He's persistent." She points out how the devil kept after Jesus despite two unsuccessful blitzes, and you compliment her response. Now you're chomping at the bit to discuss how the devil's persistence shows up two millennia later. You lock eyes with another participant and follow up Marge's answer with this probe:

"Bob, you've been a believer for a few years. Can you tell us how Satan has exhibited persistence in his warfare against you?"

You merit a "high five" for good intentions, but a "thumbs down" for sensitivity. Unless Bob is a blood brother or prior history has convinced you that nothing fazes him, the question is too threatening. Instead of addressing one person, frame the question so that *everyone* has a chance to respond, yet *no one in particular* is on the hot seat. For instance: *"Who can illustrate Satan's persistence from your experiences as a Christian?"*

The answer still calls for transparency, but now a group member's response is a matter of his or her choice.

To expedite openness among group members, weave personal anecdotes of your own into the study. When will participants exhibit transparency? When *you* model honesty. When *you* share on an emotional as well as cognitive level. When people can identify with *your* humanness. Only then will they perceive the group as a safe harbor in which to drop anchor.

So before you request illustrations of Satan's bulldog tenacity, tell your group, for example, how he hounded *you* for years to skimp on taxes or pad your expense account. Since these temptations themselves aren't sin, you won't lose credibility . . . so long as you aren't on Uncle Sam's latest "most wanted" list!

Unrealistic Questions—Keeping questions realistic is as important as keeping personal inquiries voluntary. Some study leaders tend to reel off questions that expect more than the average participant can deliver.

Why not ask the following questions? Because you can't answer them by direct observation or analysis of Matthew 4:1–11.

> On what other occasion in the Bible did someone fast for forty days?
> What other names does the Bible give for the devil?
> What Old Testament book did Jesus quote in His defense against Satan?
> The site for the second temptation was the pinnacle of the temple. What
>   was significant about that particular spot?

What other New Testament passages offer insights on Satan and spiritual warfare?

Since Jesus was divine, how was it even possible for the devil's suggestions to "tempt" Him? Wasn't He *above* temptation?

Prior to any given study, chances are you've spent at least an hour or two examining details of the text. You've delved into a leader's guide or a commentary for the scoop on doctrinal terms or controversial verses. I applaud your diligence. But will your group members come with the same background information or the same theological smarts simmering in their brain? Not likely. Many of them will look at the Bible text for the first time during your group meeting. At best, their preparation has involved workbook questions readily answered in the biblical text. There's a word for how to handle relevant material requiring extra-biblical research. Lecture. Briefly fill people in on the insights you've gleaned from your study that they can't get from the passage. Then begin asking realistic questions.

INCITE THE INTELLECT

Let's assume your questions are clear. Let's assume your queries aim for accuracy by sticking to the biblical text and exalting its authority. Let's assume their wording reveals sensitivity to group members. That's still not enough. What you ask must also stimulate thought.

Potent discussion questions stoke the furnace of the mind, resulting in vigorous investigation and analysis of Bible passages. Unless your probes spark thought, you'll extinguish learners' enthusiasm. Questions that drench motivation:

- *Call for a yes/no response*
- *Fetch effortless, obvious answers*
- *Elicit agreement with your predetermined opinions*

Yes/No Questions—As a Bible college instructor, I mentor students who teach youth and adults in off-campus settings. I observe their leadership of small groups. I've evaluated thousands of their original lesson plans. Want to know a telltale sign of inexperienced discussion leaders? Their lessons are littered with questions calling for yes or no replies. I post a NO LITTERING sign during my training sessions. Then I expect them to trash every question beginning with "Do," "Did," "Was," "Were," "Is," and "Are."

Here are a few questions on Jesus' temptation I've heard over the years. After each one is an effective revised version. Notice that the start of the question is usually the key.

Did Satan recognize Jesus' true identity? (Revision: What words in the text suggest Satan was aware of Jesus' divinity?)

Did God the Father show sensitivity to the Son after this skirmish with Satan? (Revision: Following this skirmish with Satan, how did God the Father show sensitivity to the Son?)

Have you ever overcome a temptation by recalling a verse or truth from Scripture? (Revision: Who can illustrate how a knowledge of God's Word has come to your rescue during temptation?)

Obvious Questions—A second way to douse the fires of learner participation is to rattle off questions in search of obvious information. If people's eyelids get stuck at half-mast when you're firing questions, maybe you're asking group members to investigate what's already apparent. Who wants to respond when the answer is clear to everyone? Such questions merely require participants to parrot back a phrase or fact from a single verse.

In most groups, the following questions on Matthew 4:1–11 would have the same effect as a dose of Sominex:

Where did this clash between Satan and Jesus occur?
How long had Jesus fasted before Satan appeared?
What did Satan say to Jesus in verse 9?
What did the angels begin to do when they appeared in verse 11?

Bible discussions engage learners when you rely more on analytical questions and less on factual queries. However, that doesn't mean you should never discuss factual Bible content. Factual assignments can challenge people when you ask them to discern a thread of data from a group of verses. These observation questions make data collection more challenging:

> *What were the three temptations thrust upon Jesus?* (Use it early in the Bible study so that people become familiar with the basic storyline.)
> *What do Jesus' responses to the three temptations have in common?* (I want group members to see Jesus brandishing the sword of Scripture during combat. Next, I'd use a follow-up assignment to help them articulate the wartime strategy Jesus demonstrated: *What principle of spiritual warfare did Jesus model for us?* Then I'd launch the application phase by asking for contemporary examples of the Word's value: *Who can illustrate how a knowledge of God's Word helps during temptation?*)

Leading Questions—There's a third way to insult rather than incite participants' intellect. It happens when we cast "leading" questions in their direction.

A leading question sags under the weight of your personal opinion or preconceived notions. How you formulate such a question actually reveals the answer you prefer to receive. Instead of encouraging people to think about a point in the text, you're asking others whether or not they agree with you.

Most leading questions I've heard call for a yes or no response, with a negative hitchhiking on the first word. Cases in point from Matthew 4:1–11:

> Don't you think the timing of Satan's attack on Jesus was significant?
> Isn't the fact that Satan tempted Him three times, not just once, revealing?

Let's pretend it's the night before your group meets. You're laboring over the lesson, writing a few original questions that you hope will shuttle people into the Bible passage for first-hand discovery of truth. You see a band of words such as "Didn't," Isn't," "Wasn't," "Aren't," and "Don't you think" loitering around the property line bordering your mind. They want to jump the fence and find a job on the front end of your study questions. But when it comes to a home in the cozy confines of your cerebral activity, they're illegal aliens. Put up NO TRESPASSING signs and add barbed wire to the fence. If they cross over, they'll nab the jobs that more thought-provoking words deserve.

Let's look back at the map to see where our trek through this chapter has taken us. We've concluded that a good discussion leader scrutinizes the wording of questions. We've examined four features of effective questions, couched in the acronym CAST: **Clear, Accurate, Sensitive, and Thought-provoking.** We've relied on examples from Matthew 4:1–11 to show proper and improper drafting of questions. We now realize that a teacher or facilitator doesn't shoot from the hip when it comes to questions. Inquiries carry explosive power when we prepare them carefully in advance.

Now that you've learned how to craft stimulating questions, you're ready for the next step. How should a discussion leader *respond* to answers learners give? What response skills and pointers can increase the quantity and quality of learner contributions?

I'm impressed! You're already asking the right questions. If you'll flip to the next chapter, I'll address them.

CHAPTER EIGHT

RESPONDING TO LEARNER PARTICIPATION

HILE LEADING A STUDY, Rita posed a question about hindrances to answered prayer. The second she finished the probe, Rita shifted her eyes away from group members to the Bible and sheet of notes in her lap. Ginny shared an insight gleaned from one of the Bible verses in that week's lesson. Then Elaine started to say something. But Elaine's interest evaporated when she noticed Rita's preoccupation with her notes. After a few seconds of silence, Rita supplemented Ginny's answer with a different truth from the Bible passage. It was the same point Elaine had excavated from the text, but Elaine had planned to illustrate the truth from her own experience.

✳   ✳   ✳

Brad peppers his adult Sunday school lesson with thought-provoking questions. He picks the best ones from a leader's guide, then adds a few of his own probes. That's why the absence of stimulating discussions in his class puzzles him. What answers he receives are terse. Seldom does anyone piggyback on the first response.

"Why aren't they more responsive?" Brad wonders aloud during a breakfast appointment with David. David, Brad's best friend and a member of the class, decides to shoot straight with him.

"You specialize in questions that incite the intellect," David explains. "They're so analytical that it takes a little while to investigate the Bible passage and cull answers. Not even your application questions are obvious. We have to reflect on personal experiences and realistic weekday scenarios before coming up with ideas."

"But that sounds like a *compliment*," interrupted Brad.

"So far, so good," David continued. "*But I don't think you're aware of how little time you give us to think after you pose a question.* No more than a couple of seconds pass before you answer it yourself. Brad, you've already thought about your questions during the week. But the rest of us haven't. Why, just yesterday you asked about the difference between remorse and repentance. I had read something on that subject, and my mind was busy formulating a response. Then before I could verbalize it, you dropped your research on us. I'd be less than honest if I didn't say that it crushed my enthusiasm."

✳ ✳ ✳

Tim goes out of his way to compliment teens' contributions during Bible study. When they answer questions, typical reactions from Tim include:

"All right."

"Excellent answer!"

"Good thinking."

"Way to go. Who else?"

However, the gushy commendations rankle Ed, a senior honor student and one of the few group members who takes God's Word seriously. He notices that Tim tosses out his kudos without regard to the quality of the answer. No matter how shallow, illogical, or fuzzy a response seems, Tim praises it, or at least accepts it without critical analysis.

"It's like he's afraid of hurting somebody's feelings," Ed told his mom. "It makes me clam up. Why should I give serious thought to a question if his praise isn't based on *what* I say?"

Do these scenarios strike a responsive chord? A discussion facilitator whose poor nonverbal communication short-changes her group. A Sunday school teacher whose fear of silence stifles adults' participation. A youth leader whose indiscriminate rewarding of answers waters down the power of verbal reinforcement. Rita, Brad, and Tim illustrate a taken-for-granted aspect of discussion leading. *A leader's behavior after posing questions is a hinge upon which first-rate discussions turn.* What we do after offering a question either expands or constricts the number *and* the quality of responses. This might be the toughest part of group leadership.

The following eight strategies help elicit learner participation. Add these pointers to your instructional repertoire, and you'll motivate rather than muzzle learners' interaction.

EXHIBIT ENTHUSIASM

In a Bible class or small group, *positive reinforcement* refers to things leaders do to reward learner participation. Perhaps the most potent reinforcement is expressing excitement over group members' discoveries. When you lead Bible discussions, people often find fresh, I've-never-thought-of-that-before insights. In response to a study question, participants may notice a truth for the very first time—especially if they're recent converts. Then they verbalize their discovery for others to hear.

What we say right after someone contributes is crucial. If the point is elementary to us, we may gloss over it, or give it only polite acknowledgment. Perhaps we nod and say, "Yes," "Okay," or "Uh-huh." Then we seek additional input with a prompt such as "Who else?" *But our verbal reaction should express fascination with the participant's discovery!* I'm not advocating mushy, superficial remarks, but I am encouraging you to speak a couple of sentences that dignify people's discoveries. Give verbal applause that recognizes a person's textual investigation. Public congratulations will encourage people to keep delving into Scripture and participating in the discussion. We need to help them build confidence in their study skills and convince them that God's Spirit *can* unveil biblical truth to them.

SHOW SINCERITY

Here's the flip side of the positive-reinforcement coin. *Temper your enthusiasm in relation to the quality of a group member's answer.* Remember how Tim reacted when his high school students answered a question? He praised them without regard to the quality of their answers. His attempt to salute participation backfired because his commendations came across as insincere.

So reserve your high praise for the best answers or for feedback that reveals critical thinking on the issue you're discussing. Also be sure to praise participants for thought-provoking questions they raise and for input that shows an honest effort to wrestle with the text.

VALUE VARIETY

A sure-fire way to diminish the impact of verbal reinforcement is repeated use of the same word or phrase. Overusing a particular reinforcer such as "Good," "Okay," or "Uh-huh" creates a bland rather than a stimulating learner environment. Voicing the same words over and over may give you a second or two to think about your next comment or question, but the sameness affects group members the same way gift-wrapped socks affect eight-year-olds at Christmas.

So be sure to vary your reactions to your people's responses. One way to do that is to use the tactic described in the next section.

POINT OUT PARTICULARS

Which part of a group member's commentary hit the bull's-eye? Or do you want to compliment effort instead of substance? *The more specific your verbal praise, the more meaningful it is.* Notice how the following reinforcements shine the spotlight on distinctive aspects of learner contributions.

- "Excellent answer, Valerie. I like the way you kept referring to Jesus' words to support your conclusions."
- "That's a provocative question, Joseph. Sometimes our zeal for God's Word shows more in the questions we ask than in the answers we give. Anyone want to take a shot at Joseph's question?"
- "Way to go, Bryan! You did a good job of putting Paul's remark in context."
- "Beth, that's good thinking. Could you repeat your answer so we can think about it a little more?" (Turn to others in the group.) "Notice how Beth unites these two episodes. The connection isn't obvious at first glance."

- "It's evident you fellows don't see eye-to-eye on this issue. But I appreciate the way you expressed your viewpoints tactfully and listened to each other."
- "I'm impressed by the way you connected this verse to last week's lesson."

By pointing out particular elements within a learner's remarks, you maintain variety and demonstrate sincerity. You prove that you listened carefully to what was said.

Win with Waiting

When you pose a question, how long do you wait before answering it yourself or rephrasing it? How many seconds elapse before you feel obligated to get things moving? Do you view silence as a threat to effective discussion, or do you understand that passage exploration and analysis require a reasonable amount of time?

Research in school classrooms offers relevant findings for Bible study leaders.

Students have very little time to think. Research shows that the mean amount of time a teacher waits after asking a question is approximately *one second!* If the students are not able to think quickly enough to come up with a response at this split second pace, the teacher repeats the question, rephrases it, asks a different question, or calls on another student. Moreover, if a student manages to get a response in, the teacher reacts or asks another question within an average time of nine-tenths of a second. . . . When teachers learn to increase their wait time from one second to three to five seconds, significant changes occur in their classrooms:

1. Students give longer answers.

2. Students volunteer more appropriate answers, and failures to respond are less frequent.

3. Student comments on the analysis and synthesis levels increase.

4. Students ask more questions.

5. Students exhibit more confidence in their comments, and those students whom teachers rate as relatively slow learners offer more responses and more questions.[1]

Good Bible study questions jump-start the mind, sparking thought about the passage and its practical implications. But when we show disrespect for silence and expect instant replies, discussion sputters.

Notice the Nonverbal

Whether you're engaged in a casual conversation or leading a Bible study, your communication comes across through three modes: *actual words, tone of voice, and nonverbal cues.* A wise communicator realizes that his message travels on all three avenues of expression. To maximize effectiveness, he packages his message in a way that utilizes all three modes.

You may be surprised at how little impact your words themselves make. Experts on communication theory insist that *how we say something packs more of a wallop than what we say.* Here's how one report breaks it down.

In a conversation or teaching situation, 7 percent of our message is conveyed through words, 38 percent through tone of voice, and 55 percent through nonverbal signals.

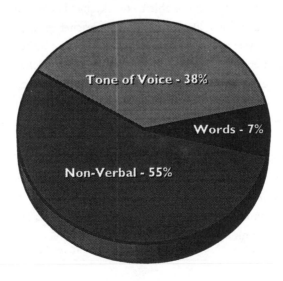

Imagine . . . both tone of voice and nonverbal signals affect the communication of our message to a much greater extent than our vocabulary! Our *nonverbal* reinforcement is significantly more potent than our verbal feedback.

When is your nonverbal communication most potent? While others in your Bible study are talking. As they answer or ask questions, what message is your body language sending? Do you come across as tense or relaxed? As interested or impatient? What you say without vibrating your vocal chords can either fan the flames of group participation or throw icy water on them.

Educational researchers have compared the relative effect of verbal and nonverbal reinforcement in response to student comments. On one occasion, college teachers intentionally sent conflicting reinforcement messages as a way of determining which mode students perceived as more powerful.

> In one group, the teacher displayed positive nonverbal reinforcement (smiled, maintained eye contact, indicated positive attitude to student answers with facial and body cues) but, at the same time, sent out negative verbal messages. In the second case, the process was reversed, and negative nonverbal reinforcement was coupled with positive verbal reinforcement (frowns, poor eye contact, and the like coupled with "good," "nice job," etc.)
>
> In both cases the nonverbal reinforcement was accepted as the primary message by the majority of students. Whether the nonverbal message was positive or negative, most students responded to the nonverbal rather than to the verbal reinforcement. This study provides fascinating support to the notion of "silent language" . . . and it emphasizes the importance of teachers attending to what they do not say as well as to what they do say as they reinforce student participation.[3]

Responding to a group member's question or input is "the art of the immediate." It's hard to prepare for because your response requires a number of complex, on-the-spot decisions. It's as much a relational skill as it is a teaching proficiency. Yet with prayerful effort, a small group leader or classroom teacher can transmit appropriate, positive nonverbal messages. Consider the following aspects of your nonverbal delivery system.

Body movement and posture—If you're a stand-up classroom instructor, expedite participation by stepping closer to the students when you pose a question. When someone responds, walk to the side of the room where he or she is speaking. Closing the gap conveys interest in what's being said. If you're sitting in the den of your home, lean forward or inch closer to the edge of your chair whenever others contribute. They'll feel that you're listening with your heart, not just your ears.

In a presentation on teaching style, Bruce Wilkinson emphasized the body's role in conveying one's feelings about the subject matter and the learners. "I have one tool to deliver my heart—my physical body. I must dedicate my body to serving my audience."[4]

Facial expressions and eye contact— In the Bible, one's "face" often represents the whole person—whether human or divine. "The LORD bless you, and keep you; the LORD make His face shine on you, and be gracious to you" (Numbers 6:24–25). When God's face shined upon Israel, He was blessing them. When He turned His face away, He was withdrawing His favor. Why did the Holy Spirit use "face" as a metaphor for the sentiments of the heart? Because without the aid of words, one's face usually expresses his inner convictions or condition.

When your group members participate in a discussion, does your face convey boredom or enthusiasm? Do you nod to let them know you're following their line of thought? Do you rivet your eyes to the person who's talking, or shift them back and forth between the participant and your notes? You may *hear* everything a group member says without looking at him. But *listening* requires eye contact.

Follow Up Their Feedback

Not all answers to your Bible study questions are fully developed. Often a group member is onto something, but his comment needs clarification. Or what she says is fine as far as it goes, but needs elaboration. Follow responses of this sort with probing questions. Your follow-up probes should spur a group member to modify or expand his initial answer, to beef up its support, to illustrate it, or to think more critically about it.

Probing for extensions of original answers is challenging. You need on-the-spot sensitivity because you can't prepare follow-up questions or comments in advance. However, just being aware that follow-up questions can be helpful is a start toward using them.

Here's a script from a Bible discussion that demonstrates the effectiveness of follow-up prompts. Notice that the leader doesn't blindly accept the initial answer. *Questions in italics* were prepared in advance by the leader. **Boldface questions and comments** indicate follow-up material inserted on the spot.

MATTHEW 4:1–11
SMALL GROUP BIBLE STUDY

Leader: Satan initially tempted Jesus to turn stones into bread (vs. 3). *What fact in this passage explains why he used food as a lure?*

Mary: Jesus was hungry.

Leader: That's correct. **But why was Jesus hungry at that particular time?**

Mary: Verse 2 says Jesus had just finished a forty-day fast. So humanly speaking, He must have been starving!

Leader: Okay. Good attention to detail. Let's build on this factual information. *What does the nature of this first temptation teach us about Satan?*

David: He's obviously pretty smart.

Leader: **What do you mean by that? Elaborate a bit.**

David: He apparently knows all our weaknesses, so he custom-designs his temptations accordingly. That seems to be what's illustrated here.

Barbara: Yeah. And if we weren't vulnerable to it, it wouldn't really be a temptation!

Leader: You've both identified an important characteristic of our enemy. He tempts us with things that obviously have appeal. He knows everyone's Achilles' heel, spiritually speaking. Let's see what else the episode tells us about the devil. *Notice that he tempted Jesus three times, not just once. What is significant about that fact?*

Joseph: Well, resisting the devil isn't a one-time thing. It's something we have to keep doing all our lives.

Leader: Absolutely right, Joseph. **But what does that imply about Satan?**

Joseph: He doesn't give up easily, that's for sure.

Barbara: Another way to put it is he's persistent.

Leader: Exactly! That's why a word picture for the Christian life is warfare. Let's keep unpacking this point. *If Satan is persistent, how should that affect us as believers?*

Mary: We need to be persistent, too. Or else we're in trouble. We won't be ready to defend against him.

Leader: Mary, you hit the bull's-eye by pointing out the basic application of this fact about Satan. But I need you to be more specific. **How does persistence show in the life of a Christian?**

In a span of several minutes, the leader employed four different follow-up probes. The range of possible follow-up questions is broad, depending on the context of the discussion. Let the following examples serve as additional catalysts for your thinking.

- **Why do you say that?**
- **Can you be more specific?**
- **What else did you notice?**
- **That term connotes different things to different people. What do you mean by it?**
- **Can you illustrate the point you're making?**
- **Do you mean . . . ?**
- **Could you rephrase your question? I want to make sure I'm tracking with you.**
- **How does that apply to . . . ?**
- **How does your answer relate to what Brad said earlier?**

Follow-up questions are only one possible way leaders can respond to an individual's participation. In the next section, we'll examine a way to respond that helps involve a greater number of group members.

Increase Involvement

Some discussions are nothing more than a question-and-answer dialog between the leader and one other participant. Only one volunteer responds to a question before the leader kicks in with either commentary or the next question. Or a group member poses a question, and no one

but the designated leader addresses it. Rarely do you hear a second participant piggyback on the initial answer someone gives. It's as if people are
afraid to trespass on the leader's domain of expertise.

A discerning discussion leader broadens the base of involvement—especially when a question has several possible answers, or during a brainstorm-
ing session on application ideas. She often encourages multiple responses to
a question before adding her own research, or going on to the next question.
When a learner asks a question, a good leader often taps the wisdom of others by redirecting the question to them. The more mature and biblically literate your study group, the more you should strive to expand learner
participation.

Which statement below distinguishes *your* Bible discussions?

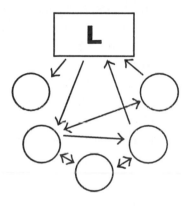

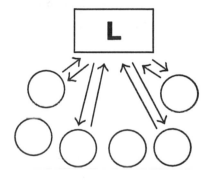

1. Participants respond to one
   another, not just to the leader.
   Leader is a facilitator.

2. Two-way conversations between
   leader and one other group
   member. Leader is considered
   the only expert in the group.

Before you supplement a group member's answer or tackle someone's
question yourself, increase involvement and interest by asking questions
similar to the following:

- **Would someone else like to address Bob's question?**
- **What do the rest of you think?**

- **Bob, you seem puzzled by Stan's comment. What's your reaction to what he said?** (Normally, I direct a question to individuals only when their expression warrants it.)
- **Jenny identified an important principle in this chapter. Who can illustrate the consequences of either obeying it, or neglecting it, in our relationships?**
- **I appreciate your transparency, Myra. Your question stems from a sincere desire to honor the Lord in that situation. Who has a biblical perspective or personal experience that can help Myra sort out her Christian responsibility in this predicament?**

In this chapter, we've discovered that the leader's behavior after posing a question is a key to learner participation. Evaluate your discussion procedures in view of the eight strategies described on the last few pages. It will have the same effect as squirting WD-40 on a rusty, squeaky door hinge. You'll open the door—*smoothly*—to a more invigorating Bible discussion. And you'll be on your way to leading powerful, life-changing studies!

Even if you excel in response techniques, leading Bible discussions still isn't a piece of cake. Do you know how to foil foes such as monopolizers and tangents? How to cover controversial content? How to rescue group conversations from the threat of relativism and uninformed conclusions? Chapter 9 takes a stab at those impediments to successful interaction.

CHAPTER NINE

Overcoming

Discussion Problems

HE WEEKLY BIBLE STUDY began with comfortable predictability. After the customary pie, the members got cups of coffee and settled into their familiar niches around the room. Charlie, the leader, cleared his throat to signal that things were starting. As he did with merciless regularity each week, he began with the question, "Well, what do these verses mean to you?"

The discussion followed a familiar pattern. Each person responded with what the verses meant to him or her, and the group reached its weekly general consensus—at least on the easier verses. They all knew what was coming, however: another stalemate between Donnell and Maria. Donnell had been a Christian for several years and was the self-appointed, resident theologian. For some reason he always seemed to lock horns with Maria, a relatively new Christian, yet an enthusiastic student of the Bible.

The scene repeated itself every time they came to a difficult verse. Donnell would argue vehemently for the interpretation of his former pastor, which usually seemed a bit forced to the rest of the group. Maria, being new and perhaps more straightforward than other group members, would challenge Donnell. Because she didn't know the Bible that well, she would relate the difficult verse to her Christian experience in a way that contradicted Donnell's interpretation. Donnell would only grow more vehement.

The stalemate usually ended with Charlie, the leader, or Betty, the peacemaker, bringing "resolution" to the discussion. One of them would calmly conclude by saying, "Well, this is another example of how reading the Bible is a matter of personal interpretation and how a verse can mean one thing to one person and something else to another." The group members would leave with a vague, hollow feeling in their chests.[1]

That small-group scenario unveils typical problems that surface when an untrained leader employs discussion. Despite the numerous advantages of Bible discussions (see Chapter 1), we must acknowledge the pitfalls. Adversaries to effective interaction include conflicting interpretations; comments rooted in ignorance or speculation rather than textual investigation; a group member who's harder to turn off than Niagara Falls; and the participant who likes to chase rabbits and tries to take everybody else along for the hunt.

If a doctrinal controversy, somebody's far-fetched interpretation, a monopolizer, or a tangential discussion sabotages a lesson you worked hard on, don't rail against the discussion format. By using the following discussion-leading techniques, you'll prevent some predicaments and exercise damage control over others.

(I realize that at this particular time, you may not be facing the specific problems that I'll address on the next few pages. If that's the case, just skim the material for now. This chapter vividly illustrates the fact that this text is a handbook. You'll want to keep it in an accessible place in your home or office, referring back to specialized content as a need arises in your teaching ministry.)

CONTROLLING CONTROVERSIES

When it comes to theology or biblical perspectives on contemporary issues, Christians don't always see eye to eye. Here are several strategies to keep disputes from demolishing your discussion.

1. Anticipate participants' questions—View each Bible lesson from the vantage point of your group members. What questions are they apt to have about interpretation or application of thorny issues in the text? Identifying in advance the passage elements that may arouse or confuse them will spur you to do your homework. This principle of anticipation amounts to a "head-them-off-at-the-pass" approach to preparation. To use it successfully, you must become as familiar with your learners as you are with lesson content.

Are you taking a diverse group of adults through Ephesians? Expect questions or firmly entrenched opinions on "predestination" (Eph. 1:5, 11), spiritual gifts (Eph. 4:7–12), and the nature of a wife's submission (Eph. 5:22). Are you touring Mark's gospel with a group of new believers? Figure on somebody's getting tripped on the unforgivable sin in Mark 3:28–29.

Anticipating group members' reactions to the text prepares you for the next strategy.

2. Set the stage for discussion with lecture—Even in a more informal discussion group, some passages or topics need the light provided by background research. Giving several minutes of historical context or another form of scholarly spadework doesn't formalize the Bible study, but it does keep participants from the snare of speculation and fruitless verbal exchanges.

Are your teens tracking Paul's advice in 1 Corinthians? You'll come across 1 Corinthians 5:5, where Paul "delivers over to Satan" a church member involved in sexual immorality. Insead of asking, "What do you think this means?" delve into a commentary. Be ready to *tell* them what Paul meant. Reserve interpretation questions for truths people can identify by observing and analyzing passage content.

Is your church mini-flock stalled in Mark 13, Jesus' Olivet discourse? Not even a Bible college class could sort out all the references to the "abomination of desolation" (v. 13), the tribulation (v. 19), or falling stars (v. 25) without a lecture to provide an interpretive framework. Try giving the two or three most recognized explanations of a passage, and the rationale for each. Then point out the interpretation you or your church prefers. All of which leads to our third way to control controversies.

3. Agree to disagree—No matter how convincing you sound, not everyone will adopt your interpretation of difficult passages. Yet you don't want the Bible discussion to bog down. A sound approach is an up-front admission of the complexity of the content. Make the following comments: "For centuries, sincere Bible scholars have viewed this doctrine differently. Though it's an important issue, we aren't going to resolve this controversy to everyone's satisfaction today. Perhaps the wisest approach is to 'agree to disagree,' and move on to other material."

Agreeing to disagree leads you to the next suggestion.

4. Set a strict time limit for group coverage of the subject matter—A troublesome point may surface in the context of a passage that offers lots of other important truths. Remember that the guiding mechanism for your lesson is the main theme or basic teaching of the passage as a whole—*not* one problematic phrase or verse. It's easy to spend an inordinate amount of time on an area of disagreement, while neglecting practical instruction that *isn't* up for debate.

For folks who still hunger for more meat on the issue, read on.

5. Recommend resources—Reference books and other extra-biblical sources shouldn't be the exclusive domain of ministerial professionals. Encourage inquisitive group members to enlist the expertise of scholarly authors.

In a doctrinal course at a Reformed church, questions erupted when we examined the doctrines of predestination and election. To supplement my lecture, I suggested they go to the church library and check out J. I. Packer's *Evangelism and the Sovereignty of God.* For learners eager to dig deeper on an issue, I've also recommended these volumes: R. C. Sproul's *Essential Truths of the Christian Faith* (Tyndale); Larry Richards' *The Teacher's Commentary* (Victor Books) and *Bible Difficulties Solved* (Revell); Charles Swindoll's *Growing Deep in the Christian Faith* (Multnomah); Bruce Wilkinson and Kenneth Boa's *Talk Thru the Bible* (Nelson); plus Warren Wiersbe's *The Bible Exposition Commentary: New Testament,* Volumes 1 and 2 (Victor Books). Books of this sort baptize you in background material without drowning you in a deluge of academic trivia.

If group members continue to clash over controversial content, consider one other strategy.

6. Minimize misunderstandings—In rare instances, class or small group participants get hot under the collar during discussion of a doctrine or social issue. One person throws a verbal jab at another, and before you know it, emotions erupt and impede logical thinking. Members move from disagreeing to being disagreeable. The mercury in the atmospheric thermometer plunges. Folks who have enjoyed friendly fellowship suddenly act like frosty foes.

Sometimes folks quarrel because they don't really listen to each other. What they perceive as a disagreement may actually be a misunderstanding. The following is an example of how to proceed if you sense that the source of the heated exchange boils down to a communication problem, or you feel that the sides aren't as far apart as they think.

Elaine and Reneé (staunch pro-lifers) are in a verbal scuffle over abortion protests. "How far should a Christian go in preventing access to clinics?" is the question on the floor. You act as a referee and send the young ladies to their respective corners. Then you say, "Elaine, summarize in your own words what you hear Reneé saying." When Elaine finishes, you ask Reneé to restate Elaine's stance as she perceives it. If either has misinterpreted the other's viewpoint, this exercise should clear up the misunderstanding.

What if the restatement of viewpoints exposes genuine disagreement? Call a halt to the discussion and allow for a "cooling down" time. Don't allow personal attacks or a harsh tone of voice. If the topic merits the time, ask Elaine and Reneé to prepare talks on their respective positions, to be given in the next group meeting. Set a time limit, with opportunities for questions from other group members. Staging an informal debate may result in a more restrained, rational discussion of the different opinions. In the end, you'll probably want to encourage all involved to cordially agree to disagree. (See strategy 3.)

MANAGING MONOPOLIZERS

Every now and then you'll encounter a group member who feels that a second of silence is a divine mandate to speak. Though most monopolizers are motivated learners who are passionately involved with the subject matter, their verbal initiative can cause passivity among others in the group. Here are ways to increase the percentage of group members who participate.

1. Introduce a study question with a qualifying remark—I've received lots of mileage out of this one: "The next question should be answered by someone who hasn't contributed yet today." (Except I wouldn't use it if the group consisted of only two or three persons!)

2. Set specific conditions for learner response—Examples: "I appreciate the responsiveness of ladies in the group. Men, now it's *your* turn to answer the next couple of questions." "The next question must be answered by someone to my right (or someone in the last four rows, whose birthday falls in the spring, etc.)."

3. Give a couple of group members who don't monopolize conversations a question or assignment a week in advance—At the appropriate time during the next Bible lesson, ask them to report on their research. Select individuals who possess a high regard for Scripture and who you can count on to follow through. In the case of teens or relatively new believers, maintain quality control by assisting them in the assignment.

4. Plan for a variety of discussion strategies or forms—For instance, divide a larger class into small buzz groups. Give the smaller groups a specific assignment in the Bible text, and a time limit. Tell every small group to appoint a recorder who'll later summarize the group's findings for the whole class. Mixing the question-answer approach with other forms of discussion broadens participation and may muzzle monopolizers.

5. Speak one-to-one with the monopolizer—If the person's talkativeness is prompted by enthusiasm for learning, make comments similar to the following: "John, you're the kind of learner I'd like to photocopy and put in every chair! But I need your help in getting others as involved in discussions as you are. Because they expect *you* to respond, they're shifting into a passive mode and aren't wrestling with the questions. I want you to keep participating. But could you delay your answers to some questions and compel your peers to get more involved?"

DRAINING THE POOL OF IGNORANCE

I've heard folks criticize Bible discussions because they "degenerate into a pooling of ignorance." The critics say learners often "create meaning" rather than stick to the correct interpretation of the text. Let's face it: The nemesis of relativism does show up at some of our Bible studies. Yet there are ways to block its entrance and safeguard against uninformed conclusions cropping up in the study.

1. Prepare the Participants—Ignorance evaporates when *all* participants commit to old-fashioned study of the Bible passage. Determine a reasonable amount of "homework" time and ask members to sign a covenant. Devoting thirty minutes to the passage prior to each session won't turn them into scholars, but it may prompt them to shuck preconceived notions. When you meet, they'll already have some rapport with the biblical text.

Another option is to employ published materials. Look for a Bible study curriculum providing student workbooks as well as leader's guides. An alternative is to prepare study questions yourself and distribute them a week ahead of time. When you meet, incorporate the homework questions into the publisher's (or your own) more extensive lesson plan. Let's look at an example of how this could work.

In Mark 5, three people experienced Jesus' life-changing power: a demoniac, a woman with an issue of blood, and Jairus' daughter. A week prior to the study on this passage, I gave group members the following questions:

- **What effects did Satanic influence have on the man?**
- **What words/phrases in verses 6-15 show Jesus' superiority over Satan?**
- **How would you describe the way the main characters approached Jesus with their needs?**
- **What characteristics of Jesus can you find in these three episodes?**
- **What trait of Jesus illustrated in Mark 5 means most to you right now? Why?**

2. Qualify the questions—The verb "qualify" means "to reduce from a general to a particular or restricted form." That's what you want to do as you prepare study questions. Narrow the scope of possible answers by wording questions in a way that directs learners' attention to the Bible text. I call this the "let-the-text-be-the-teacher" approach to discussions.

The following are examples of questions that allow the text, not human opinion, to sit on the throne of authority. I plucked the questions from a lesson on King Uzziah from 2 Chronicles 26. Notice how the wording keeps the spotlight on the text.

- **From verses 1–15, what words/phrases show that King Uzziah was a success?**
- **What reasons for his success can you find in these verses?**
- **How did Uzziah react to his success and fame?**
- **How did his pride show?**
- **What were the consequences of his proud spirit?**
- **What timeless insights about pride does this biblical case-study offer?**

3. Enlist the Experts—Some Scripture passages are difficult to interpret without the insight provided by a sound commentary or Bible encyclopedia. Instead of soliciting learners' opinions, do your homework and lecture for several minutes. Otherwise you put out the welcome mat to ignorance and usher it to a front row seat in your class.

It's critical that leaders study Bible passages on their own and avoid excessive dependence on somebody else's research. Yet a leader must not rely solely on his or her own findings and ideas. *The group leader who learns only from himself has a fool for a teacher!*

4. Mix the Members—Whenever you divide into smaller clusters for Bible discussions, don't approach the allocation of members indiscriminately. A typical collection of learners consists of both "new and used" Christians. John and Mary came to Christ six months ago, without one iota of church background. Leslie and Rhonda joined the church back in the Jurassic era. They've sat at the feet of good teachers for several decades. In each small group, put a more biblically literate person with two or three newer believers. Or assign a young adult sponsor to each buzz group of teens. Set up your groups so that the less-mature participants will profit from others' experience.

If you're afraid your learners will drown in the deep waters of uninformed conclusions, drain the pool using the strategies we've just examined. Pull the plug by preparing the participants, qualifying your questions, enlisting the experts, and mixing your members.

RESCUING RABBITS

"Chasing rabbits" is an analogy describing the activity of participants who steer a discussion off course. Those nose-twitching, rascally varmints don't run in a straight line. They zig and zag, bolt right, then left, making it difficult for even a sportsman the caliber of Elmer Fudd to hit them with buckshot. When a member of your group darts after rabbits, the direction of the discussion gets derailed.

The word for this problem is "tangent." It's a deviation from the intended course. Any remark that digresses from the study slant or is irrelevant to the topic or Bible passage is a tangent. Minimize tangents—and give those hares a hiatus from hunting—with the following suggestions.

1. Search for a Slant—From a single Bible lesson your group may glean numerous truths. But as you prepare, and while leading the discussion, don't examine various points in isolation from the larger picture provided by the passage. Your observation and analysis of the text (see Chapters 3 and 4) should help you identify an overarching, unifying theme. Clearly communicate the broad theme that governs the passage, and participants will be less likely to steer the conversation away from it. Connect the facts and principles to a comprehensive subject slant, and group members' ideas or illustrations will usually mesh with it.

Jim Wilhoit and Leland Ryken salute the importance of a single focus for a Bible lesson.

> Symptomatic of inability to deal adequately with a biblical text is the prevailing failure to identify the "big idea" of a biblical passage. The "big idea" is the thought that unifies a biblical passage and that ought to govern a class session. Ineffective teachers tend to focus on isolated facts and to present their audience with a stream of unrelated ideas in the dim hope that if they throw out enough ideas a few will stick.[2]

Call it the *big idea, theme statement, basic teaching, a thesis sentence, the proposition, the main thought*—the concept is the same. The point is to subordinate details of a Bible passage to a broader theme. Provide a general, organizational framework that gives your lesson coherence and connects various parts of the passage.

Let me share three brief examples.

NEHEMIAH 1

The chapter opens with Nehemiah's inquiry about the Jewish remnant in Jerusalem. When he hears of their discouragement and the decimated walls, Nehemiah weeps, fasts, and prays. In the prayer he hails God's attributes, confesses sin, quotes promises God made to Moses, and appeals for divine intervention.

The chapter offers several lessons for the contemporary reader, but every conclusion can be linked to a unifying theme: *the ministry of intercession.* Want to shine the spotlight on Nehemiah's character traits? To emphasize his inquisitiveness? His sensitivity? His self-discipline? Explain how these qualities serve as prerequisites for a ministry of intercession. Without the qualities Nehemiah modeled, intercession is no more than a good intention.

Want to highlight Nehemiah's memorization of sacred promises concerning Israel? Connect his Bible knowledge to the broader context. Show

how an awareness of Bible content—especially of God's promises—motivates us to intercede for others.

2 CHRONICLES 26

Early in his reign, King Uzziah sought and obeyed the Lord, and God rewarded him with material and military success. But prosperity went to Uzziah's head, and pride prompted him to take a casual attitude toward God's law. He burned incense in the temple, a duty God had reserved for the priests. As a result, God struck Uzziah with leprosy.

The snare of pride provides a unifying framework for investigating this narrative. Treat evidences of Uzziah's success in verses 1–15 as the *cause* of pride. Prosperity poses a stiff test of faith for any believer. Uzziah's corrupt behavior demonstrates how pride leads to moral erosion, and the blight of leprosy shows the negative consequences of a proud spirit. Uzziah's story illustrates Proverbs 16:18: "Pride goes before destruction, and a haughty spirit before stumbling."

THE LIFE OF BARNABAS

To obtain cash for the church in Jerusalem, Barnabas sold a farm (Acts 4:32–37). He later defended a zealous Jewish convert named Saul in front of skeptics in the same church (Acts 9:26–28). Sent as an emissary to a new congregation in Antioch, Barnabas spent a year grounding the church in the truth about Jesus. To accelerate the discipling process in Antioch, he recruited Saul (later named Paul) to work alongside him (Acts 11:19–26). After an adventurous missionary trek with Paul, he stood up for a young fellow who had deserted them. When he and Paul didn't see eye to eye, Barnabas severed ties with him and accompanied the young man—John Mark—to Cyprus (Acts 15:36–41).

Whether you plan several studies on Barnabas or skim all the events in a single lesson, stitch the episodes with a common thread: *the ministry of encouragement.* Encouraging others apart from selflessness and sensitivity is impossible. Barnabas' character qualities provided fertile soil for his lifestyle of concern for others. In Acts 4, he encouraged the church by releasing his resources. He encouraged new converts in Antioch by activating his abilities and mobilizing others to exercise their spiritual gifts. By pardoning their past, and vouching for their potential as servants of Christ, Barnabas encouraged Paul (Acts 9) and John Mark (Acts 15).

With enough hard work, almost anyone can come up with a unifying theme for a passage. But hard work *is* involved in discovering a theme yourself. And you may not have extra hours each week to spend in detailed biblical analysis. Fortunately, there's another way to find that unifying theme: Pluck a resource book or published curriculum off the shelf of a Christian bookstore. Let the scholars trumpet a theme for you, then organize your questions around it. No matter who gives birth to the basic teaching or "big idea," it keeps everyone on track.

The simplest way to zero in on a theme is to keep the following questions in front of you during preparation.

- **What are the most significant facts in this passage?**
- **When I analyze these facts, what timeless truths or principles for living emerge?**
- **How can I keep from treating the various facts and truths in isolation from one another?**
- **What ideas, instructions, or actions appear in each segment or episode?**
- **How does all this material connect or fit together?**
- **What themes or threads of thought surface?**
- **What single theme or topic dominates or governs the text as a unit?**

Focusing on a single theme leads logically to a second tangent-busting suggestion.

2. Polish Your Probes—To what extent do your questions unify the lesson? Do your queries show participants the main idea of the Bible passage? Does the wording of questions on specific passage elements connect those insights to the big picture?

Before we look at the role of questions in unifying a passage, read the first chapter of Nehemiah.

1 The words of Nehemiah the son of Hacaliah. Now it happened in the month Chislev, in the twentieth year, while I was in Susa the capitol,

2 that Hanani, one of my brothers, and some men from Judah came; and I asked them concerning the Jews who had escaped and had survived the captivity, and about Jerusalem.

3 And they said to me, "The remnant there in the province who survived the captivity are in great distress and reproach, and the wall of Jerusalem is broken down and its gates are burned with fire."

4 Now it came about when I heard these words, I sat down and wept and mourned for days; and I was fasting and praying before the God of heaven.

5 And I said, "I beseech Thee, O LORD God of heaven, the great and awesome God, who preserves the covenant and lovingkindness for those who love Him and keep His commandments,

6 let Thine ear now be attentive and Thine eyes open to hear the prayer of Thy servant which I am praying before Thee now, day and night, on behalf of the sons of Israel Thy servants, confessing the sins of the sons of Israel which we have sinned against Thee; I and my father's house have sinned.

7 "We have acted very corruptly against Thee and have not kept the commandments, nor the statutes, nor the ordinances which Thou didst command Thy servant Moses.

8 "Remember the word which Thou didst command Thy servant Moses, saying, 'If you are unfaithful I will scatter you among the peoples;

9 but if you return to Me and keep My commandments and do them, though those of you who have been scattered were in the most remote part of the heavens, I will gather them from there and will bring them to the place where I have chosen to cause My name to dwell.'

10 "And they are Thy servants and Thy people whom Thou didst redeem by Thy great power and by Thy strong hand.

11 "O Lord, I beseech Thee, may Thine ear be attentive to the prayer of Thy servant and the prayer of Thy servants who delight to revere Thy name, and make Thy servant successful today, and grant him compassion before this man." Now I was the cupbearer to the king.

Now examine the two sets of questions that follow. The first list lacks a unifying theme. But notice how the second group of questions keeps the focus on "the ministry of intercession."

NEHEMIAH 1:1–11
(NO CLEAR, UNIFYING THEME)

1. What news did Nehemiah receive about the people in Jerusalem? How did he react to the news?

2. Nehemiah wept in response to the conditions in Jerusalem. When is weeping a sign of weakness? When does a person's weeping signify strength?

3. Verses 5–11 summarize Nehemiah's prayer. How would you describe this prayer?

4. How does Nehemiah describe God? Why is awareness of these divine attributes important?

5. In verses 6–8, what is significant about the term "we"?

6. What is Nehemiah confessing?

7. How does Nehemiah's Scripture quotation in verses 8–9 relate to his reason for praying?

8. Who can illustrate from personal experience a benefit of Scripture memory?

9. What character qualities does Nehemiah exhibit in this chapter? (Rhetorical: Which of these character traits is most lacking in *your* life right now?)

NEHEMIAH 1:1–11
(THEME: THE MINISTRY OF INTERCESSION)

1. What news did Nehemiah receive about the Jewish remnant in Jerusalem?

2. What does Nehemiah's inquiry about the Jewish remnant teach us about the ministry of intercession?

3. Who can illustrate how inquisitiveness helps an intercessor?

4. Nehemiah wept, fasted, and prayed over the plight of the people and Jerusalem (vs. 4). To what extent does pain or brokenness fuel intercession? Who can share a time when a period of intercession was prompted by pain?

5. Verse 5 lists several divine attributes. What is the correlation between these particular attributes and the ministry of intercession? How does one's view of God affect the practice of prayer?

6. In verses 6–8, what is significant about the term "we"? Why is identification with the needs or plight of others important to an intercessor?

7. How does Nehemiah utilize a knowledge of Scripture in his prayer?

8. What effect can an awareness of Bible content have on our practice of intercession? Who can illustrate how a verse or truth from Scripture prompted you to pray for someone?

9. From his words and actions in Chapter 1, what else can we learn from Nehemiah about intercessory prayer?

10. Which insight about intercession is most helpful to you right now? Why?

11. What are some concrete tips or strategies for beefing up our ministry of intercession?

3. Build a Bridge Back—Imagine you're smack dab in the middle of a Bible discussion. Someone inserts a personal illustration or comment that seems extraneous. Though the connection is unclear, something in the Bible text or prior conversation likely sparked the contribution. Why else would the participant utter it? How can you dignify the person's remarks and still convey the importance of sticking to the subject matter?

Try asking the contributor to build a verbal bridge back to the passage slant or topic. Perhaps an explanation of what triggered the tangential material will reveal the connection to everyone. Here are methods I've used to get a group back to the topic.

- *Tom, what you said is interesting, but tell us how it relates to the topic (or Bible passage) we're discussing. What connection do you see?*
- *Betty, thanks for contributing. But I'm curious. What part of the Bible passage triggered your comment?*
- *Sally, thanks for the transparent nature of your illustration. What made you think of it? Was it something one of us said? Or a verse we examined?*

Tactfully asking questions of this sort won't always result in a verbal bridge that passes inspection. Yet your effort will train group members to evaluate their contributions for pertinence.

The advice in this chapter isn't a cure-all for doctrinal controversies, monopolizers, eccentric interpretations, or tangents. But if you heed the tips, *your* group members won't leave with a vague, hollow feeling in their chests. In direct contrast to Charlie's group leadership in the opening anecdote, you'll minimize the pitfalls and maximize the benefits of Bible discussions.

✳   ✳   ✳

If I glanced at your business card, would the title "Pastor" or "Director of Christian Education" catch my eye? Are you a freshly minted "Small Groups Coordinator" for a church launching a new emphasis on fellowship? A Sunday school superintendent responsible for teachers of teens and adults? A parachurch professional with the task of nurturing staff who lead group Bible studies? A missionary executive serving in a field ripe with a mushrooming number of "cell group" churches? A Christian school administrator who supervises classroom teachers of Bible?

If you wear any of these hats, Appendices A and B will prick your interest. You'll digest time-tested concepts on leadership development. And you'll find a detailed *Leader's Guide* to facilitate your ministry of training Bible study leaders.

For Trainers of Teachers and Small Group Leaders

Growing New Bible Discussion Leaders

EVERY TIME I TAKE a new course, attend a seminar, or read a book, his words resurface. He spoke them over two decades ago, in an address to the student body at Wheaton Graduate School. But his remark still goads me into action. The moment I become slothful about what I've learned, fail to convey to others what has benefitted me, or hoard the training I've received, the statement echoes in my memory. What did pastor and author Stuart Briscoe say that holds me accountable?

**God never blesses or teaches you
solely for you own benefit!**

That's all I remember from his hour-long message. But God's Spirit has stamped the sentence deeply into my consciousness, reminding me that I'm a channel through which the Lord wants to educate others in the body of Christ. When I unpack the maxim, I realize I'm not merely called to teach God's Word. Better yet, I'm to train others so *they* can teach the Bible. Here's how Paul put the principle: "The things which you have heard from me . . . entrust to faithful men, *who will be able to teach others also*" (2 Tim. 2:2, italics mine).

Ever wish you could be in two places at once? The closest you'll ever come to it is cultivating an *equipping mindset* in your area of ministry. By passing on the concepts and competencies you acquire, you add to the Lord's labor force. Mason Roberts reminds us why we use the term *reproduction* synonymously with *training:* "When you get a hundred individuals to do 1 percent more than they would have done without you, you have created a new life."[1]

By now you know where I'm going with all this. *Don't just lead successful Bible discussions. Keep an eye out for folks you can train for a similar ministry.* Apply the concepts, preparation strategies, and presentation tactics gleaned from this book in a two-fold manner: first, to improve your own teaching; second, to prepare additional small group leaders and Sunday school teachers.

On the following pages, two resources are available to assist in your development of other Bible study leaders. Here in Appendix A we'll examine seven concepts integral to any training ministry and explore how each principle pertains to the specific sphere of developing discussion leaders. In Appendix B, you'll find a leader's guide for taking a group of trainees through this book.

LEARNING HOW TO LEAD

How does a person learn to teach or lead group Bible studies? Acquiring any ministry skill involves three primary processes:

- Training
- Observing
- Practicing

Training is the instruction and assistance you receive from a mentor or experienced leader. It's the acquisition of knowledge plus know-how that serves as a prerequisite for honing a skill. Training takes a variety of forms: attending a leadership development course or seminar, reading a book, watching a how-to video, or participating in one-on-one discipleship, to name a few.

Observing is the intentional effort to learn from a model. You watch as an experienced leader demonstrates the skills you hope to acquire.

Observation is a specific aspect of the broader concept of training. You're more apt to perfect a skill if you repeatedly see it exhibited.

Practicing is a rehearsal of the skill you hope to develop. To increase the likelihood of success, practice should occur in a supportive setting, with evaluative feedback from a supervisor.

The first letters of the three key words spell T-O-P. Applying these three processes to your development of workers should result in "*top*-notch" lay leadership. Mull over this question: *How can I incorporate all three processes in my training of Bible discussion leaders?*

TEAM BUILDING

One distinguishing factor between a church group and a business or civic organization should be the nature of relationships. That's why "team building" is an integral part of your agenda for church training events. *team building is any structured or intentional effort to improve the experience of fellowship among participants.* The time you reserve for team building isn't an appendix to your meeting or an optional warm fuzzy. Rather, it's what sets your group apart as *Christian.*

Start a file of mixers, get-acquainted games, and creative activities that promote sharing and increase familiarity among trainees. Two sources of ideas are books you read and workshops you attend. Whether you come across an idea while reading, or you're present when someone else implements it, jot down the procedure and keep it for future use. (For examples in this book, see Chapter 2, plus Sessions 1 and 9 in Appendix B.)

EQUIPPING VS. EXPOSING

What Bruce Wilkinson said about Bible teaching applies to leadership training: "We wrongly believe that a greater quantity of content covered is better than a greater quantity of content learned."[2] To put it another way, *less is sometimes more.* What counts isn't the amount of material you cover; it's the amount learners can grasp and apply during a session. Frequently we provide more material than participants can successfully assimilate.

Ask yourself: *What are the implications of this principle for my training of Bible discussion leaders? Am I exceeding their "cognitive speed limit" by zooming through these concepts and skills? Would a more deliberate pace encourage questions and make skills-practice a top-shelf priority? Am I flexible enough to devote an extra week to a topic, even if the consequence is omitting something else entirely?*

How you answer those questions determines whether you're *exposing* workers to the material, or *equipping* them to lead. (Appendix B provides an example of this principle. It contains *two* sessions on Chapter 4, "Preparing Interpretation Questions." The analytical nature of this material is too challenging for only one hour of coverage.)

SHOWING VS. TELLING

Years ago I attended a nationally-advertised Christian Education conference. I had circled in my program the workshop I most eagerly anticipated: "Better Bible Discussions." But I left the session disenchanted instead of excited. The only instructional method the workshop leader utilized was lecture. Not once did he pose a question. Not once did he demonstrate the teaching skill he urged us to develop.

In any training session, *our methodology must match the message we're delivering.* The learning process we employ is as important to participants' training as the content we convey. Why? Because acquiring a skill is virtually impossible without first observing a model. *We do what we see, not what we hear.*

Think of the teachers/small group leaders you're training. *Are you modeling for them the concepts and skills you're covering in the sessions? Are you showing them—not just telling them—what to do and how to do it? Are they experiencing as learners the kind of relational climate and questioning skills that you expect them to implement as leaders?*

If your answer to these questions is *yes*, there's no *telling* how far they'll go as discussion leaders!

STRUCTURING FOR SUCCESS

Tom wanted to meet weekly over breakfast to go over Bible study methods. "I want to know how to discover things on my own," he insisted. He asked for homework, accountability, evaluation of his work—the whole nine yards! The first week, I showed him how to outline a Bible book. His assignment? To identify a major theme in Philippians, then construct an original outline showing how each part of the epistle reflected that theme.

The second method I introduced was an observation chart (see Chapter 3). He categorized various facts and threads of information found in Philippians 1. Both his original outline and completed chart smacked of diligence. "If only everyone were this motivated!" I thought privately.

Then Tom said something I'll never forget. "You should have started me on the observation chart instead of the outline." When I pressed for his reasons, Tom said, "Going through Philippians from start to finish—showing how each part correlated with the theme—took hours! And the process wasn't as easy for me as you made it seem. I almost canceled our second meeting. I wasn't at all sure if I was on the right track. But the observation chart—that was something I could handle. I got excited about all the stuff I was seeing in the passage!"

Tom went on to say that the complexity of outlining would have been easier to take if he had previously succeeded with a simpler study method. Starting with a difficult assignment made him feel dumb and inadequate. But the observation method boosted his self-confidence and improved his attitude toward Bible study.

In capsule form, here's what Tom taught me about leadership development: *Success motivates.*

No matter who I'm nurturing in spiritual disciplines or ministry skills, I ponder these questions: *How will my placement of concepts and skills within the training sequence affect participants' attitude toward learning? To instill a sense of competence, which discipline or ministry skill should I put first? During training sessions, what can I say or do to increase people's potential for success? How should this motivational concept affect the roles we give inexperienced volunteers? Do some church positions or age-level ministries increase the prospect of failure for a first-timer? After trainees launch a ministry, what kind of support network will accelerate their experience of success?*

When you apply those questions to your training of discussion leaders, what kind of answers do you get?

THE TRAINING CYCLE

Transferring a ministry competence or leadership proficiency from one person to another requires a fixed series of operations.

- I CAN DO IT. The leader has experience and some degree of expertise in the skill to be imparted.
- I DO IT, WHILE OTHERS WATCH. The leader demonstrates the ability. By observing, others pick up nuances and procedures that accelerate their acquisition of the skill.
- WE DO IT TOGETHER. The leader delegates a limited amount of responsibility to others. Leader and learners plan and implement an event or method as a team. The apprentices gradually gain self-confidence. The difficulty and amount of their responsibility increases in small increments.
- THEY DO IT, WHILE I WATCH. The leader becomes the observer while learners go solo. The leader stays around to offer encouragement and evaluative feedback.
- THEY DO IT. (And the cycle keeps repeating itself!)

How does this training cycle apply to your development of Bible study leaders?

EVALUATING PROGRESS

Fred Smith asks himself five questions to evaluate the progress of people he trains. He has applied these criteria to church responsibilities as well as the corporate world.

1. *Is this person's job fitting well with his or her talents?* If not, I haven't got a prayer of developing that person to his potential.

2. *How much willingness to do the job am I seeing?* I watch to see if the person is enthusiastic about opportunity, if this work is more than just something to fill the time.

3. *How consistent is the person's effort?* Long-term, day-in, day-out effort is what pays off in an organization. You don't want someone who does things only when he feels like it.

4. *What are the objective results?* A lot of people give you lots of activity, conversation, excuses—but if you really measure what they've done, you find little.

5. *Is this person willing to be evaluated?* I'm not going to spend my time developing somebody who resists having his results measured. . . . It's not easy to evaluate a teacher, I admit, but it's not impossible.[3]

Use these questions to evaluate people you're training. And use Appendix B to equip small group leaders and teachers in discussion-leading skills.

Lesson Plans for Training Sessions

WHAT FOLLOWS are twelve start-to-finish, hour-long training meetings based on Chapters 1–9 of this book. The lesson plan for each training session follows the **Approach-Absorb-Apply** format described in Chapter 6. The subsections within each major division of the lesson plans correlate with the wording of subheads in the pertinent book chapter.

Every lesson is chock-full of questions and other learning activities. Rather than merely rehash content in the book chapter, trainees evaluate their Bible study leadership in light of the recommended discussion procedures. In a hands-on fashion, they practice preparation strategies as well as presentation techniques. And they pray for one another's ministries. Whenever you hold training sessions, establish the kind of learning environment you want to characterize their groups. Demonstrate the lesson format and questioning skills you want them to employ. *They'll learn as much from the process you model as from the content you cover.*

Though the *Leader's Guide* calls for weekly meetings over a three-month period, think of ways to adapt its content. Perhaps a half-day seminar format is more realistic for your small group leaders or Sunday school teachers. Merely select a couple of chapters from the book and zero in on those concepts or skills. A few months later, cover one or two new topics. Here's one layout for training discussion leaders over a twelve-month period, utilizing the half-day seminar arrangement.

HALF-DAY TRAINING FORMAT
(4 DAYS, SPREAD OVER SCHOOL YEAR)

AUGUST
8:30–10:00 **Creating a Climate for Discussion**
(*Caring, Laughter, Intercession* sections of Chapter 2)
10:00–10:15 Coffee Break (Freshly brewed fellowship!)
10:15–11:45 **Creating a Climate for Discussion**
(Remainder of Chapter 2)

OCTOBER
8:30–10:00 **Preparing Observation and Interpretation Questions**
(Chapters 3–4)
10:00–10:15 Coffee Break (Perk up!)
10:15–11:45 **Preparing Application Questions** (Chapter 5)

JANUARY
8:30–10:00 **Organizing Your Discussion Plan** (Chapter 6)
10:00–10:15 Coffee Koinonia
10:15–11:45 **Guidelines for Effective Questions** (Chapter 7)

APRIL
8:30–10:00 **Responding to Learner Participation** (Chapter 8)
10:00–10:15 Coffee Koinonia
10:15–11:45 **Overcoming Discussion Problems** (Chapter 9)

Whatever organization format you select, see to it that every participant gets a copy of *You Can Lead a Bible Discussion Group*. Reading a book chapter in tandem with a training session will facilitate leaders' absorption of the material.

Session 1—Team-Building and Introduction

SESSION AIMS
- To create a warm, relational climate among teachers or small group leaders.
- To dispel a prevalent myth about leading Bible discussions.
- To identify the components of effective Bible discussions.
- To preview the topics covered in this training course.

APPROACH (15–20 minutes)

Instruct group members to take an item from their wallet or purse that communicates something personal or distinctive about them: a photograph; receipt; ticket stub from a professional ballgame or movie; keys; business card—you name it! Divide participants into smaller groups of four to six people. They will tell why that item is important or what it says about their past, their personality, or priorities. Encourage others to probe for additional information as a means of getting better acquainted. (*How long have you worked in real estate? How did you meet your husband?*) To give people a sample of the creativity and self-revelation you're after, display and explain *your* selection in front of everyone.

Before moving to the next phase of the session, distribute copies of *You Can Lead a Bible Discussion Group.*

ABSORB (25–30 minutes)

TAKING DISCUSSION FOR GRANTED

Everyone you've assembled for this training session is either a small group facilitator for whom questioning is the primary instructional strategy, or a Bible teacher whose repertoire of methods includes discussion. So it's important to address a misconception many folks have about the relative ease of discussion methodologies.

Read aloud the anecdote featuring Randy (first two paragraphs in the "Taking Discussion for Granted" section of Chapter 1). Discuss:

- **What is your reaction to Randy's comment? Why?**
- **What do you think accounted for his "discussion-is-easier" attitude?**

Next, refer participants to the "Taking Discussion for Granted" section of Chapter 1. Ask them to read silently the remaining paragraphs. The consequence of Randy's casual attitude is twofold: He fails to prepare sound questions in advance, and he's blind to the potential pitfalls of Bible discussions. Point out that the book and these training sessions enable leaders to meet head-on the challenges of Bible discussions.

DEFINING DISCUSSION

Walk participants through this part of Chapter 1. Spend several minutes dissecting the one-sentence definition of "discussion." Put the definition on a poster or an overhead transparency so everyone's attention is fastened on it as you discuss these questions:

- **What factors make a small group or classroom "hospitable"?**
- **How does the learning environment either generate or stifle discussion?** (After several respond, point out that the next book chapter and training session offer strategies for creating a hospitable environment.)
- The term "guided" is used to describe conversations that occur during a group Bible study. **What is significant about that word?**

TRACKING TOPICS

This section of Chapter 1 previews the subject matter of the book and this course. Give people a couple of minutes to skim the questions that will be addressed. Ask: **Which question (or set of questions) are you most eager to cover? Why?**

Listen carefully to participants' feedback. Their responses constitute felt needs in the areas of Bible study preparation and discussion leading. Allow what they say to shape the slant of future training sessions and the amount of time you spend on a particular topic. Adapt this *Leader's Guide* to the distinctive needs of your group. The ideas should stimulate your thinking, not replace your originality. Perhaps you'll skip one of these lesson plans altogether and devote extra time to a skill or concept you deem especially important.

APPLY (12–15 minutes)
  Share the following quote with participants:

  God's work, apart from prayer, at best produces clever ineffectiveness.[1]
  —W. E. Sangster

  Close with a time of intercessory prayer. Invite everyone to voice specific requests he or she has as a group leader or teacher. Ask another individual to pray for each need that's voiced. Model the transparency you're after by sharing specific requests regarding your leadership of these training sessions. Show leaders that it's okay to feel dependent or in need of wisdom.

LOOKING AHEAD
  Assign the remainder of Chapter 1 plus Chapter 2 of *You Can Lead a Bible Discussion Group*. The next session identifies eight benefits of Bible discussion and introduces the first three of seven strategies for improving the learning atmosphere of study groups.

SESSION 2—BENEFITS AND CLIMATE BOOSTERS (CHAPTER 1)

SESSION AIMS
- To list the benefits of employing discussion in a group Bible study.
- To identify three ways to create a group atmosphere that fosters interaction.
- To have each participant commit to specific strategies for enhancing the climate of his/her study group.

APPROACH (6–8 minutes)

Ask several volunteers to describe a benefit of Bible discussions they've experienced in a study group. Tell them to share specific anecdotes. To provide transition into the heart of the session, point out that awareness of discussion dividends increases the likelihood of experiencing those dividends. This session explores the advantages of discussion, then shifts the spotlight to group characteristics that promote stimulating interaction.

ABSORB (30–35 minutes)

DETERMINING DIVIDENDS

Chapter 1 of *You Can Lead a Bible Discussion Group* examines eight potential dividends of discussion-oriented Bible study. Take a couple of minutes to review verbally the eight benefits. Then use the following questions to piggyback on participants' reading of this material.

- **Which of these benefits are you most eager to experience in your group? Why?**
- **Which dividend of discussion has been rarest in study groups or classes you've attended? Why do you think that's the case?**

Also, pose one or more of the following questions regarding specific benefits. Which ones you select will depend in part on the responses you receive during the introduction to this session.

- **Who can share a time when verbal interaction taught you something significant about group members' needs or attitudes?**
- **Who can share a time when significant mutual ministry occurred during group interaction?**
- **Who can illustrate how a learner's contribution during discussion added to your knowledge of the Bible passage or subject matter?**

Next, refer participants to the six criteria (six questions) for spotting potential leaders on page 11. Challenge them to look for potential leaders in their class or group. Encourage them to channel names of such people to you for possible follow-up.

Read aloud Ephesians 4:11–12 and 2 Timothy 2:2. Emphasize that leaders are equippers, not just teachers. Remind them that prospective group leaders will receive valuable training merely by observing them in action!

CREATING A CLIMATE FOR DISCUSSION

Chapter 2 describes seven climate-boosting strategies. You'll examine the first three in this training session: *caring, laughter,* and *intercession.* Increase participants' ownership of these three ideas with the following questions and activities.

CARING

- **Why is a caring environment crucial to successful Bible discussions?**
- Read Philippians 1:3–11 and 1 Thessalonians 2:7–11. **What words or phrases from these passages indicate that Paul developed close relationships with people he served?**
- The author offers practical tips for cultivating a caring environment (pages 15–17). **What other ways can a leader express concern for group members?**
- **How else can we improve relationships among group members?** (You'll find questions of this sort dotted throughout these lesson plans. Participants' experiences provide an important supplement to ideas in the book.)

LAUGHTER

- What is your reaction to the section on humor? Why?
- To what extent is the teacher or facilitator responsible for invoking laughter?
- What kinds of humor are inappropriate for Bible study groups?
- What limitations or restrictions would you impose on a leader who seeks to inject humor into group meetings? Why?

INTERCESSION

- What benefits does intercession bring to Bible discussions?
- What are obstacles to significant intercession among group members? How have you worked to overcome these hindrances?
- The author offers three ways to enhance intercession in a study group (pages 19–20). What other strategies have you implemented or observed?

APPLY (12–15 minutes)
- In a time of conversational prayer, ask volunteers to thank God for benefits of discussion already experienced by his or her group. Invite others to entreat Him so the dividends not yet experienced will materialize in the near future.
- Divide into pairs. Refer participants to the concrete, transferable tips for climate building sprinkled throughout the first three sections of Chapter 2 (get-acquainted mixers, intercession projects, etc.). Ask everyone to select one or two of these ideas that he can implement within the next few weeks. Then everyone can pray for his partner's follow-through.

LOOKING AHEAD

Encourage participants to read through the remaining sections of Chapter 2 of *You Can Lead a Bible Discussion Group*. To whet their appetite for four additional climate-boosting strategies, read aloud the quotation by Ray Stedman on page 27. Tell people they'll discover the correlation between a leader's transparency and the learning atmosphere of the group.

SESSION 3—MORE CLIMATE-BOOSTING STRATEGIES (CHAPTER 2)

SESSION AIMS
- To discuss guidelines for selecting group Bible study methods.
- To enumerate ways to help guests experience a sense of belonging.
- To pinpoint the value of and restrictions on a group leader's personal disclosures.
- To identify ways to improve the physical environment of a study group.

APPROACH (12–15 minutes)

Chapter 2 describes three new get-acquainted activities: *designer name tag; name acrostic;* and *nonverbal introductions.* Begin this session by implementing one of those activities with trainees. This will serve two purposes: enhance relationships among course participants and demonstrate a tool they can use in their groups or classes. They're more apt to use an idea they experience than an idea they just read about.

ABSORB (30–35 minutes)

METHODOLOGY

- **How is knowing the recent history of a group and the leadership style of your predecessor helpful to your preparation?**
- This section of Chapter 2 uses the acronym M-E-T-H-O-D-S to introduce seven guidelines for selecting learning activities. **Which guideline did you find most helpful? Why?**
- **What additional methods criteria do you recommend?**
- "Discussion" is a broad term that takes numerous forms. **What variations in discussion methodology have you implemented or observed?**
- **When is a brief lecture necessary to set the stage for meaningful discussion?**
- **How should the presence of non-Christians in a Bible study affect methodology? The nature of questions you ask?**

ASSIMILATION

- Ask a couple of volunteers to describe a time they visited a small group or Sunday school class, but chose not to return. Ask: **What kept you from going back?**
- To reinforce the importance of assimilating guests into a Bible study group, read aloud the following research findings. What church-growth leaders discovered about adult Sunday schools applies to home Bible studies, too.

Several intriguing research studies support the fact that people's participation in Sunday school depends on the existence of or the lack of relationships.

One such study found that the number of close friends a person develops in the Sunday school has a direct relationship to that person's own involvement in the Sunday school. If a person has few or no close friends in the Sunday school, the chances are quite low that he will be active in the Sunday school. If an individual has many close friends in the Sunday school, that person will be more active.

The importance of friendship in the Sunday school can be seen in another study. It compared fifty new members who were still active six months after joining with fifty new members who dropped out after six months. The new members who stayed and were incorporated had each made more than seven new friends in the church and Sunday school. Those who dropped out had made fewer than two.

Additional evidence which shows the importance of the relationship between friendship and successful assimilation comes from interviews with Sunday school dropouts.

People were asked: 1) why they dropped out of Sunday school, and 2) what would most influence their choice of a new church home. The answer regularly given to question number one was "Did not feel part of the group." The response to the second question, given by a majority of the people, was "Friendliness of the people."[2]

- The book describes a "class host" position for adult Sunday schools. **In what other ways can we utilize members of our groups or classes to help assimilate guests?**

- **What effective assimilation strategies have you personally observed or implemented?**

TRANSPARENCY

- Think of a Bible teacher or group leader who has demonstrated the trait of transparency. **What effect did this person's self-disclosure have on you as a Christian?**
- **Why does a leader's initiative in self-revelation tend to encourage honesty on the part of others in the group?**
- Review the six guidelines for self-disclosure on pages 26–27. **Who can share a time when you or a teacher you heard disregarded one or more of these guidelines?**
- **What are the potential consequences of indiscreet disclosures?**
- This part of Chapter 2 concludes with questions that promote openness among group members. **Which of these questions are you most likely to include in your lesson plans? Why?**

ENVIRONMENT

To explore this variable, invite participants to complete these sentences:

- Ways to enhance the physical settings of study groups include

  _____.

- Sometimes we're in a physical setting that we can't change. Ways a sharp leader can compensate for an undesirable setting include

  _____.

APPLY (10–12 minutes)

Use the acronym C-L-I-M-A-T-E to review the seven factors that foster discussion. (Three factors were covered previously, then four more in this session.) Then form triads. Instruct everyone to identify the climate-boosting factor that is *already most prominent in his or her group.* (Together, thank God for the presence of that group characteristic.) Next, ask everyone to reveal the climate-boosting strategy *most lacking in his or her group.* (Intercede for one another's action plans for improving in these areas.)

LOOKING AHEAD

Read aloud the one-sentence quotation from Fred Smith at the start of Chapter 3. Emphasize that the next few sessions zero in on aspects of preparation. Participants will learn how to investigate a Bible passage and ask stimulating questions about the text. Assign Chapter 3 of *You Can Lead a Bible Discussion Group*.

SESSION 4—PREPARING OBSERVATION QUESTIONS (CHAPTER 3)

SESSION AIMS
- To identify the kinds of factual information that most often crop up in Bible passages.
- To gain a sense of competence in the observation phase of Bible study through group practice and mutual encouragement.
- To articulate guidelines for selecting facts that merit coverage during group Bible studies.

APPROACH (3–5 minutes)
Launch your meeting by reading aloud the follow anecdote:

A small bottle containing urine sat upon the desk of Sir William Osler, the eminent professor of medicine at Oxford University. Sitting before him was a class full of young, wide-eyed medical students, listening to his lecture on the importance of observing details. To emphasize his point, he announced: "This bottle contains a sample for analysis. It's often possible by tasting it to determine the disease from which the patient suffers."

He then dipped a finger into the fluid and brought it into his mouth. He continued speaking: "Now I am going to pass the bottle around. Each of you please do exactly as I did. Perhaps we can learn the importance of this technique and diagnose the case."

The bottle made its way from row to row, each student gingerly poking his finger in and bravely sampling the contents with a frown. Dr. Osler then retrieved the bottle and startled his students by saying, "Gentlemen, now you will understand what I mean when I speak about details. Had you been observant, you would have seen that I put my index finger in the bottle and my middle finger into my mouth."[3]

Emphasize that observing details is crucial to Bible study, just as it is in medical diagnosis. Today's session covers the "observation" phase of study, and how it applies to successful group discussions.

ABSORB (40–45 minutes)

FOCUSING ON FACTS

Review the two definitions of "observation." One definition relates to Bible *study*. The second defines it in reference to *a phase of group discussion*. Discuss:

- **Why is the *observation* phase of Bible study so vital?**
- **When a group meets for Bible discussions, why is there a tendency to skip or minimize the observation phase of study?**

FINDING THE FACTS

Give participants several minutes to review this section of Chapter 3. The observation chart is a tool that identifies the kinds of factual information most often found in passages of Scripture. Be sure people have read the explanation of each observation cue. Before you proceed, field questions they have about the method.

Prior to your meeting, put the observation chart on 8 ½" x 11" paper, using the format on page 34. Of course, leave proportionate space for writing so participants can use it as a worksheet. Make enough copies to give every person at least two blank sheets.

Give learners a feel for observational Bible study by working on a Bible passage together: *John 15:1–17.* Time may not permit you to finish the worksheet during the session, but you can demonstrate the chart's usefulness by assigning everyone two or three columns. Divide the columns among trainees so at least the following observation cues are covered: *Who; What; Commands; Cause-effect; Repetitions; Contrasts.* Give people twelve to fifteen minutes to fill in their assigned columns. Then go over the findings together. Compliment their attention to detail. Point out that it's too early to determine the significance of these facts. Such analysis is part of the next phase of Bible study: *interpretation.* The purpose today is to discover how to use the chart as a means of collecting factual data.

Emphasize that the observation chart is a *preparation tool* for leaders who want to investigate a passage in depth. They won't have time to employ the chart every week, yet occasional use will train their eyes to spot important information. Normally, they won't employ the worksheet during group studies they lead, but the data they record on the worksheet will help them formulate observation questions for the group time.

APPLY (12–15 minutes)

FORMULATING FACTUAL QUESTIONS

The ultimate application of the completed observation chart comes during the interpretation phase of Bible study. At this juncture of the course, apply the data collected on John 15:1–17 by covering the "Formulating Factual Questions" section of Chapter 3.

Review the guidelines for selecting observation questions: *to preview the passage; to pinpoint patterns;* and *to inform interpretation* (pages 39–42). People may need time to skim these sections again. Instruct them to work in pairs and write several factual questions for John 15:1–17 that meet the selection criteria. (For example, here's a question that pinpoints a pattern of passage data: **What words or phrases are repeated numerous times in these verses?**)

Go over participants' "practice" questions as a group. Explain that a future book chapter and training session will give tips for wording questions. Right now, your purpose is twofold: (1) to show people how to distinguish between important and unimportant facts, and (2) to practice formulating questions that will enable their study groups to discover the important facts.

LOOKING AHEAD

Tell participants to finish the observation chart on John 15:1–17 and bring it to the next session. Assign Chapter 4 of *You Can Lead a Bible Discussion Group.* Point out that finding the facts of a Bible passage is a means to an end, never an end in itself. The next book chapter and training session show how to analyze the observations from John 15:1–17.

Session 5—Interpreting a Bible Passage (Chapter 4)

SESSION AIMS
- To clarify the difference between an observation and an interpretation of a Bible passage.
- To explain the four-step procedure for moving from observation to the interpretation phase of Bible study.
- To practice the four-step procedure by analyzing observations from John 15:1–17.

APPROACH (8–10 minutes)
Participants were asked to finish the observation chart on John 15:1–17. Give them an opportunity to report on their findings.

- **Which observation column (type of factual information) was most helpful for your data collection?**
- **Who can share a fact or thread of information in John 15 that you uncovered since our last meeting?**
- **What lingering questions do you have about observing a Bible passage?**

Make transition into the interpretation phase of study and explain that this session and the next will reveal what to do with all the passage data.

ABSORB (40–45 minutes)
Due to the difficulty of the interpretive process, devote two sessions instead of one to this subject matter. This session focuses on the formulation of truths from a Bible passage. The next meeting shows how to write analytical questions so *others* can discover the same truths. Going too fast through this material will result in *exposure*, instead of training.

INTRODUCING INTERPRETATION

Put the analytical phase of Bible study in a broader context by reviewing the three phases of study and teaching:

- *Observation:* What does the passage *say?*
- *Interpretation:* What does the passage *mean?*
- *Application:* What is the *significance* of this passage for our lives?

To expand on the definition of "interpretation," ask: **In your own words, what is the difference between an *observation* and an *interpretation?*** To solidify participants' understanding, review the author's explanation as needed.

SIMPLIFYING THE STEPS

Verbally review the four-step procedure for analyzing a text: **prayer; probes; precepts;** and **proofs.** Be sure people have read the sample probes and precepts from Matthew 4, Mark 5, and Deuteronomy 6. Discuss:

- Notice the correlation between the four timeless truths (precepts) and the factual material from which they stem. **How would you describe this connection?**
- **Why is a close connection between an interpretive statement (precept) and factual content important?**
- Notice the kind of questions the author asks himself about each set of facts. **How would you describe these mental probes?**
- **What impresses you most about this peek at his reasoning?**
- **According to the author, how do we confirm or test the validity of a conclusion?**
- **What can we learn from these examples that will enhance our own interpretation of passages?**

PRACTICING THE STEPS

Each person will need a Bible and his observation chart on John 15:1–17. Divide into pairs. First, go over the "Interpreter's Prayer" together on page 47, substituting plural pronouns for singular ones. Then instruct everyone to point out what he considers important facts, or data trends, in the passage. Together, pairs should work through the four-step procedure in the "Simplifying the Steps" section of Chapter 4. Encourage people to brainstorm or "think out loud"—especially during the process of probing the facts for meaning. Ask each pair to formulate at least two precepts (interpretation statements) from John 15:1–17. Allot twenty to twenty-five minutes for their work, and let them know you're available for consultation as they wrestle with the passage.

APPLY (10–12 minutes)

Before dispersing, ask several volunteers to articulate a truth they gleaned from John 15. Because they observed the passage before analyzing it, you'll probably receive sound conclusions, but ask every respondent to explain how passage facts support the precept. Enthusiastically affirm valid insights. You want people to feel excitement over their personal discovery of truths.

LOOKING AHEAD

Next week's session is based on the "Guiding Your Group" section of Chapter 4. Tell participants to review this material on writing interpretation questions and to pay careful attention to the samples provided. Ask them to apply it at home by constructing a couple of questions based on precepts in John 15:1–17. Their questions should be ones they would use if they were leading a discussion on the passage.

SESSION 6—PREPARING INTERPRETATION QUESTIONS (CHAPTER 4)

SESSION AIMS
- To discover guidelines for sound interpretation questions.
- To practice writing interpretation questions for John 15:1–17.
- To appraise each other's interpretation questions in light of the guidelines in Chapter 4.

APPROACH (2–3 minutes)
Read aloud the following statement:

The art of questioning . . . is the art of guided learning.[4]

Emphasize that a discussion leader is a *guide* to others' learning instead of a transmitter of information. This session on interpretation questions shows people how to lead others on a safari into God's Word.

ABSORB (45–50 minutes)
This meeting correlates with the "Guiding Your Group" section of Chapter 4 and focuses on writing interpretation questions.

GUIDING YOUR GROUP

Last week participants worked in pairs to analyze factual information in John 15:1–17. You asked them to review the "Guiding Your Group" section of Chapter 4 at home and to prepare several questions based on their analysis.

Instruct them to work with a partner again—the same partner as last week if possible. Tell them to exchange questions and evaluate each other's probes in light of the checklist of criteria on page 53. The verbal feedback they give one another will sharpen trainees' analytical abilities.

Then give people time to formulate additional interpretation questions on John 15:1–17. After twenty-five to thirty minutes, tell each pair to select from their list the *two* questions they like best, and have partners share those questions with the whole group. After each twosome reports, encourage others' assessment of the questions by asking: **Which question do you think is**

better? Why? How can the wording of the questions be improved?
(Note: If the setting for your training session is a classroom, give each pair a
blank sheet of transparency film and a transparency pen. Have pairs project
the samples for all to see. Visualizing their questions will enhance the evaluative feedback.)

OPTIONAL IDEAS FOR THIS SESSION

- Prepare five or six interpretation questions of your own from John
  15:1–17. Distribute copies of your probes and ask for participants'
  feedback in light of the guidelines on pages 52–55.
- Bring copies of a lesson plan from a curriculum manual or published
  Leader's Guide. Any Bible passage or topic will suffice. Ask your
  group to use content in Chapter 4 to evaluate the interpretation
  questions in the printed material. (Your workers won't always write
  their own lesson plans. Yet the training they're receiving will enable
  them to adapt published lessons or supplement them with questions
  of their own.)

APPLY (8–10 minutes)

So far you've employed John 15:1–17 as a "practice" passage for observation and interpretation. Jesus' teaching in those verses teems with life-
changing truths. To conclude, shift the focus from the skills you're
developing to the *message* of John 15:1–17.

- **Which truth from John 15:1–17 impresses you most? Why?**
- **During your investigation of this passage, how has the Lord spoken to you personally?**

LOOKING AHEAD

Read aloud:

"Interpretation without application is abortion of the Word of God."

Assign Chapter 5. The next session shows how to move a Bible study
group from analysis of a passage to its life implications.

SESSION 7—PREPARING APPLICATION QUESTIONS (CHAPTER 5)

SESSION AIMS
- To show how the application phase of group Bible study differs from observation and interpretation.
- To identify a method for personal application of a Bible passage.
- To examine the mental process of connecting Bible content to the daily lives of group members.
- To practice formulating questions that predispose learners to application.

APPROACH (3–5 minutes)
  Read aloud:

> *The Bible wasn't given for our information but for our transformation.*[5]
> —Dwight L. Moody

- Ask: **How should Moody's statement affect the way we prepare and lead Bible studies?**

Since the ultimate goal of Scripture is life change, we cannot take for granted the application phase of lessons. The aim of transformation influences how we prepare as well as present group Bible studies. Instead of leaving it to chance, we're responsible to teach for application.

ABSORB (45–50 minutes)

LINK LESSONS TO LIFE

Ask a volunteer to define the phrase *"teaching for application."* Refer to the commentary in this section of Chapter 5 as needed.

The remainder of this session examines a five-step approach to teaching for application.

Step 1: Personalize the Passage
This section lists seven questions for a devotional study of a Bible passage. Leaders who filter a text through their own lives will more likely weave

application into their lessons. Give participants several minutes to mull over John 15:1–17 in light of these seven questions. Their previous spade work in the chapter should minimize the time required for this exercise. Ask several volunteers to share their responses to any of the questions.

Now tell people to imagine they're preparing for a group discussion of John 15:1–17. Ask: **Which of these devotional questions would you include in your lesson? Why?**

Step 2: Connect Content to Contexts

Review the questions that help a leader think in terms of learner application. Emphasize that "teaching for application" is first and foremost *a way of thinking* about the Bible in terms of group members' needs.

Step 3: Ask for Anecdotes

Give participants several minutes to review this application strategy. Tell them to pay careful attention to the examples from Matthew 4, Mark 5, and Deuteronomy 6. Ask them to return to John 15:1–17 and write one personal question seeking illustrations of a truth. After each volunteer reads aloud his personal question, solicit feedback on it.

Add the following examples of anecdotal questions. To help learners experience the value of such probes, instruct them to actually respond as if you were teaching John 15:1–17.

- **Who can illustrate from experience a benefit of "abiding in Christ"? A consequence of failing to abide?**
- A dominant theme in these verses is fruit bearing. John refers to "fruit" (vv. 1, 2), "more fruit" (vv. 1, 2), "much fruit" (vv. 5, 8) and "fruit [that] should remain" (vs. 16). Let's focus on fruitfulness in the context of church ministry. **Who can illustrate the difference between *apparent* fruitfulness and *lasting* fruit?**
- Wrap up this phase of your session with this question: **How does illustrating a Bible truth expedite application?**

Step 4: Probe for Possibilities

This type of application question is future oriented. Learners link the lesson to life by identifying conceivable outcomes of truth. They describe the effects obedience would have on typical slice-of-life situations.

Once again, review the sample probes from Matthew 4 and Deuteronomy 6. Then form smaller teams of three to four persons. Instruct teams to formulate questions for John 15:1–17 that address behavioral applications of specific principles. When you bring the groups back together, ask a representative from each team to share the questions they wrote. Add the following examples to their lists:

- **If a believer is "abiding in Christ," in what ways will it show in his or her schedule?**
- Imagine a non-Christian is spending lots of time with a group of Christians over a period of several weeks. **If those Christians are "loving one another," what kind of things is the unbeliever observing?**

Before moving to the APPLY segment, point out that "probing for possibilities" conditions learners to think *specifically* about biblical principles. They leave group meetings with concrete response ideas instead of vague generalities.

APPLY (10–12 minutes)

Step 5: Learn Your Limitations
- **What limitation does a Bible study leader face regarding application?**
- **How does a leader express dependence upon the Holy Spirit?**

Tell everyone to find a prayer partner. Exchange prayer requests concerning the small group/teaching ministry each person leads. Pray for one another's needs as leaders and for specific burdens each person has for members of his study group.

LOOKING AHEAD
Say: *Another way to "teach for application" is to utilize a discussion plan format that accentuates response. The next session explains a step-by-step approach to Bible lessons that requires us to reserve time for application.*
Assign Chapter 6.

Session 8—Organizing Your Bible Discussion (Chapter 6)

SESSION AIMS

- To identify the distinguishing characteristics of each segment of a discussion plan: **Approach the Word; Absorb the Word;** and **Apply the Word.**
- To lead a thirty- to thirty-five-minute Bible study during which you demonstrate the three segments of a discussion plan.

TRAINING STRATEGY

During the first thirty to thirty-five minutes, lead your trainees through a Bible study on a single passage of Scripture. Your purpose is to demonstrate the organizational format described in Chapter 6, plus the types of questions explained in Chapters 3–5. Start with an interest-grabbing approach activity, employ observation and interpretation questions in your investigation of Scripture, and pose two or more questions that spur people to think about application.

Don't tell participants in advance that you're planning a demonstration discussion. Just proceed with the Bible study. Bring extra Bibles to the session or reproduce the passage so everyone will be working from the same translation.

When you finish, use the following questions to analyze your demonstration.

APPROACH THE WORD

- **Why is an "Approach the Word" segment necessary at the start of a group discussion?**
- **How did I introduce the Bible study?**
- **Did my "Approach" activity accomplish its purpose? Why or why not?**

ABSORB THE WORD

- **What is a discussion leader's responsibility during the "Absorb the Word" lesson segment?**

- During our investigation of the Bible passage, what different kinds of questions did I ask?
- Which question most effectively pried open the text for you? Why?
- In Chapter 6, the author recommends writing your own answers to the study questions you plan. Why?

APPLY THE WORD

- How did I help you connect the Bible content to your life experiences?
- Which question was most effective in helping you think about life response? Why?
- According to the author, we may weave a few application questions into the "Absorb the Word" segment. Not all lessons will segregate all application questions from the process of Bible investigation. **Why is flexibility in the placement of application probes important?**

Give people copies of the discussion plan you used in the demonstration. To facilitate their own implementation of the recommended structure, be sure it contains the same terminology and procedures described in Chapter 6.

LOOKING AHEAD

Ask for examples of poorly worded Bible study questions. Then emphasize that it isn't enough to pose a combination of observation, interpretation, and application questions. We also must word every question in a biblically and educationally sound manner. The next session offers tips for constructing good questions. Assign Chapter 7 and *ask people to bring all the material they've accumulated so far on John 15:1–17.* Persons currently leading a Bible study should also bring their notes or published lesson plan for their group meeting that immediately follows the next training session.

SESSION 9—GUIDELINES FOR EFFECTIVE QUESTIONS (CHAPTER 7)

SESSION AIMS
- To identify four features of effective Bible study questions.
- To recognize the most common mistakes leaders make in their wording of questions.

APPROACH (6–8 minutes)
Begin with one or more of the following discussion starters:

- **What about the guidelines for writing questions offered in Chapter 7?**
- **Don't you think the section in Chapter 7 on relativism in group discussions is significant?**
- **Since the author lists numerous mistakes leaders make in wording questions—mistakes that probably crop up in our own lessons—which problem with wording is most common, based on your own experience in observing and leading Bible studies?**
- **Are questions that call for just a "yes or no" response common in Bible studies you attend?**

Of course, these questions break specific guidelines in Chapter 7! Ask: **Which wording criterion did the question(s) I posed transgress?** Point out that this session helps them learn more about writing sound questions.

ABSORB (40–45 minutes)

REVIEWING THE GUIDELINES

Employ a question-answer approach to review the features of successful questions and the most common mistakes in wording. Refer to the pertinent pages in Chapter 7 as you proceed.

- **How does the author help us remember the four basic features of good questions?**
- **Which foe of clarity do you think is most common in Bible discussions?**

- **Which foe of accuracy do you most frequently encounter during Bible studies?**
- **Why do so many leaders pose speculative questions?**
- **What makes a Bible study question "irrelevant"?**
- **What is "relativism" as it relates to Bible discussions?**
- **What's the difference between a truth's "meaning" and its "significance"?**
- **Who can illustrate the use of an insensitive question during a Bible study?**
- **What makes a study question realistic as opposed to unrealistic?**
- **When is a question thought provoking?**

APPLYING THE GUIDELINES

Select one of the following learning activities:

(A) Have participants form pairs and go over questions they previously wrote for John 15:1–17. Encourage them to evaluate those probes in light of the wording criteria in Chapter 7 and to work together to revise specific questions as needed.

When you reconvene, ask several persons to report on a question they revised. Tell them to read the original question, describe the revision, and identify the wording guideline that influenced them.

(B) Select this alternative if most of your trainees currently teach a class or lead a small group. Have people work in pairs to go over each other's Bible passage and discussion plans for the upcoming study. Evaluate all questions in view of the guidelines in Chapter 7, revising them as necessary. If leaders utilize published materials, they can appraise the questions provided. Tell participants to determine if any question breaks a guideline and to identify probes that best reflect the distinguishing features of good questions. If leaders don't have their next Bible study planned yet, they can use this time to prepare original questions that meet the standards.

APPLY (10–12 minutes)

Remember to cultivate within training sessions the kind of learning environment you want leaders to develop within *their* study groups. Close with the following team-building activity.

Have people share the title of a magazine that describes their life over the past week. Have them explain the reasons for their selection. Spur their thinking with these examples:

- *Decision*—"I'm wrestling with the possibility of changing jobs."
- *Changing Times*—"We're still adjusting to our last kid going off to college, marveling at how the past few years zoomed by."
- *Money*—"My wife just went to work so we could pay for our kids' tuition!"

Pray together for the needs and burdens revealed by the periodical titles.

SESSION 10—RESPONDING TO LEARNER PARTICIPATION (CHAPTER 8)

SESSION AIM
- To demonstrate tactics for reinforcing or extending group members' participation in discussion.

APPROACH
- **What are some social skills that come in handy during Bible discussions?**
- **Which of these skills are most needed by leaders immediately after we pose a question?**

Emphasize that our response to group members' answers, as well as to their questions, is often a taken-for-granted aspect of leadership. This facet of discussion leading calls for sharp relational skills as well as teaching know-how.

ABSORB
In Chapter 8, we explore the following specific response techniques:

Exhibit Enthusiasm
Show Sincerity
Value Variety
Point Out Particulars
Win with Waiting
Notice the Nonverbal
Follow Up Their Feedback
Increase Involvement

The most effective way to instill these relational skills and teaching tactics within your trainees is through dramatic presentations. Here's a suggested procedure.

If your group consists of sixteen or more, divide into teams of four. Assign each team *two* of the eight strategies. If you have a smaller number, determine which of the eight strategies you deem most vital to discussion leadership. Then assign each team of three to four people *two* of those ideas.

Ask each team to review the pertinent sections of Chapter 8. *Have them think of a typical Bible study situation in which the leader either models or neglects the behaviors advocated in those sections. Then have each team prepare a brief skit showing either the application or omission of each strategy.* Encourage creativity and realism. People can pretend their team is a small Bible study group and other trainees are just observers, or they can think of a way to involve everyone in the room during the demonstration. A team may incorporate both assigned strategies into one hypothetical teaching situation or give two separate skits.

After each dramatic episode, ask for feedback to this question: **What discussion-leading skills were omitted or applied?**

APPLY (8–10 minutes)

Ask everyone to identify the positive behavior or response strategy he feels is most lacking in his group leadership. In a time of intercession, ask a different volunteer to pray for each need that was expressed.

LOOKING AHEAD

Ask: **What are some difficulties or problems you've experienced during group Bible discussions?**

Point out that the next session tackles four typical challenges to successful discussions: monopolizers, tangents, controversies over doctrine, and a "pooling of ignorance." Assign Chapter 9.

Session 11—Handling Discussion Problems (Chapter 9)

SESSION AIM
- To identify strategies for controlling controversies, managing monopolizers, minimizing tangents, and discouraging a "pooling of ignorance."

APPROACH (5–7 minutes)

Ask participants to skim the opening anecdote in Chapter 9. Discuss: **How would you describe the leadership of this group?** After several respond, point out that an effective group leader can prevent or minimize most discussion-related problems. This session shows how.

ABSORB (40–45 minutes)

CONTROLLING CONTROVERSIES

- **What cultural trends and congregational characteristics make unanimity on matters of interpretation increasingly rare?**
- **What doctrinal questions and controversies most often surface in your study groups?**
- **Which strategy for controlling controversies do you consider most helpful? Why?**
- **What is the value of a strict time limit for group coverage of controversial content?**
- **When is it wise to insert a brief lecture into a Bible discussion?**

MANAGING MONOPOLIZERS

- **What motives or factors prompt someone to monopolize a Bible discussion?**
- **What effect does a monopolizer have on others in the group?**
- **In Chapter 9, which technique for muzzling monopolizers impresses you most? Why?**
- **In what additional ways can we increase the percentage of group members who participate?**

DRAINING THE POOL OF IGNORANCE

- Imagine you meet someone who says that a Bible teacher's role is to dispense information. He disdains discussion because "people just display their ignorance." **How would you respond to this person?**
- The author encourages us to "prepare the participants." **To what extent is homework realistic in our study groups?**
- **What should characterize at-home assignments that we give?**
- **How can our wording of Bible study questions either promote or restrict uninformed conclusions?**
- **During discussions, how can we utilize the more mature, knowledgeable group members to help us maintain biblical integrity?**

RESCUING RABBITS

- **What are some causes of tangential remarks during Bible discussions?**
- Neighbor Nudge: **Together, in twenty-five words or less, summarize the strategy labeled "search for a slant."** Let several trainees share their summaries. Supplement their efforts as needed.
- **How can the questions we ask either unify or segregate the parts of a lesson?**
- Review the two sets of questions on Nehemiah 1:1–11 (pages 119–120). **Explain why the second set does a better job of unifying passage elements under a single theme.**
- The author recommends asking participants to explain how their apparent tangential remarks relate to the day's lesson. **What is his rationale for this suggestion?**

APPLY (10–12 minutes)
- **What is the Holy Spirit's role in helping us overcome discussion problems?**
- **Who can illustrate how prayer and reliance on God's Spirit helped alleviate a problem in your group?**

Give participants time to describe any difficulties they're currently experiencing as group leaders. The problems may or may not correlate with the four predicaments covered in Chapter 9. Close with conversational prayer, making sure someone intercedes for every group dilemma mentioned.

LOOKING AHEAD

According to Mark Twain, *education is whatever remains when we've forgotten all we've been taught!* Read Twain's remark aloud. Point out that we're less likely to forget these training sessions if we participate in a meaningful review. The next meeting reconsiders significant ideas from the course and *You Can Lead a Bible Discussion Group.*

Session 12

Due to the uniqueness of this session, you won't find the usual step-by-step lesson format. Instead, select one or more of the following ways to review and wrap up the course.

TESTIMONIALS

Seek volunteer responses to these questions:

- **How has the training you've received affected your *attitude* toward leading Bible studies?**
- **What recent compliments have you received from learners regarding your group leadership?**
- **Which *preparation* tip from the book or course has helped you most?**
- **Which *presentation* tip has proved most useful?**
- **In what additional areas do you feel a need for training?**

TEAM BUILDING

Since we launched these training sessions . . .

- One thing I've learned about myself is
  _____.
- One person in the group I've learned to appreciate is
  _____, because _____.
- One way God has become more real to me is
  _____.
- One way others in this group can pray for me right now is
  _____.

PANEL OF EXPERTS

Invite a couple of the most experienced small group leaders or teachers from your church to serve on a panel. Also recruit one or more vocational

Christian workers in your area who have expertise in small group ministry or teaching: leaders in para-church organizations; Bible college faculty; or staff members of a different local church. Give prospective panel members a few questions in advance. Think of needs or subject areas addressed in the course that you want to cover more extensively. Or pose relevant questions about small groups or Bible teaching not tackled by the course or by *You Can Lead a Bible Discussion Group*. Reserve time for spontaneous questions from course participants.

Here are questions I've used successfully with panels:

- **What are some "vital signs of health" for a small group (or Sunday school class)?**
- **If you were training Bible study leaders, what concepts and skills would you be sure to cover? Why?**
- **If you could instantly bestow just one skill upon Bible discussion leaders, what would it be? Why?**
- **What would you tell a leader who's discouraged about the progress of his or her group?**
- **What resources—books, conferences, videos—do you recommend for Bible study leaders?**

RESOURCE DISPLAY

On a well-decorated table, display samples of books, curriculum, videos, and periodicals geared to the needs of your leaders. Ask a local Christian bookstore to loan you items to sell on a consignment basis. Arrange on-the-spot check-out of any materials available through your church library or resource center. Plug specific items you've personally found helpful. Also, distribute several highly regarded items to course participants a week in advance. Ask them to read sample chapters or articles, and review them for others during this meeting. Include in your resource display published curriculum for groups, especially leader's guides that incorporate concepts and tips covered in training sessions.

DISCUSSION DEMONSTRATION

Find a course participant who's willing to lead the group in a thirty- to forty-minute Bible discussion. Select someone who's teachable and willing to be evaluated by you and by peers. Instruct him or her to model the discussion format explained in Chapter 6, plus proper wording of questions. Offer to meet with this person during the week to assist in preparation.

After the Bible lesson, evaluate the demonstration for the benefit of everyone present. Start with affirmation, then proceed to suggestions for improvement. Discuss:

- **What were the strengths of the Bible lesson?**
- **What leadership skills did (name of person) demonstrate?**
- **What suggestions do you have for improving the Bible discussion?**

Notes

Chapter One: The Challenge and Value of Bible Discussions

1. Maryellen Weimer, *Improving Your Classroom Teaching* (Newbury Park, Calif.: Sage Publications, 1993), 49–50, 57.

2. Donald Cruickshank, Deborah Bainer, and Kim Metcalf, *The Act of Teaching* (New York: McGraw-Hill, Inc., 1995), 181.

3. Terry Powell, *Student and Faculty Perceptions of Nonclassroom Student-Faculty Interaction: A Qualitative Investigation* (Ann Arbor, Mich.: University Microfilms, 1994).

4. Jim and Carol Plueddemann, *Pilgrims in Progress: Growing through Groups* (Wheaton, Ill.: Harold Shaw Publishers, 1990), 54–55.

5. Wilbert McKeachie, *Teaching Tips*, 8th ed. (Lexington, Mass.: D.C. Heath, 1986), 83.

6. Ibid, 83.

7. Bill McNabb and Steven Mabry, *Teaching the Bible Creatively* (Grand Rapids, Mich.: Zondervan/Youth Specialties, 1990), 65.

Chapter Two: Creating a Climate for Discussion

1. Stephen Pile, *The Book of Failures*, quoted in Charles Swindoll, *Growing Strong in the Seasons of Life* (Portland, Ore.: Multnomah Press, 1983), 29.

2. Charles Swindoll, *Growing Strong in the Seasons of Life* (Portland, Ore.: Multnomah Press, 1983), 254.

3. Ann Darling and Joan Civikly, "The Effect of Teacher Humor on Student Perceptions of Classroom Communicative Climate," *Journal of Classroom Interaction* 22 (Dec.–Jan. 1987). 24–30.

4. Debar Korobkin, "Humor in the Classroom," *College Teaching* 36, no. 4, 154–58.

5. Ibid., 155.

6. Ibid.

7. Richard Lederer, *Anguished English* (Charleston, S.C.: Wyrick and Company, 1987), and *More Anguished English* (New York: Delacorte Press, 1993).

8. Ross and Kathryn Petras, *The 776 Stupidest Things Ever Said* (New York: Doubleday, 1993).

9. Jay Leno, *Headlines* (1989); *More Headlines* (1990); *Headlines III: Not the Movie, Still the Book* (1991); and *Headlines IV: The Next Generation* (1992). (New York: Warner Books).

10. Howard Hendricks, *Teaching to Change Lives* (Portland, Ore.: Multnomah Press, 1987), 150.

11. Charlotte Phoenix, "Get Them Involved! Styles of High- and Low-Rated Teachers," *College Teaching* 35, no. 1 (Winter 1987): 13–15.

12. Powell, *Student and Faculty Perceptions.*

13. Larry Richards, *A Theology of Christian Education* (Grand Rapids, Mich.: Zondervan, 1975), 142.

14. Ray Stedman, *Authentic Christianity* (Portland, Ore.: Multnomah Press, 1973).

15. McNabb and Mabry, *Teaching the Bible Creatively*, 165–74.

CHAPTER THREE: PREPARING OBSERVATION QUESTIONS

1. Fred Smith, *Learning to Lead* (Waco, Tex.: Word Books, 1986), 150.

2. *The Illustrated Sherlock Holmes Treasury* (New York: Avenue Books, 1976), 2, 17.

3. Bruce Wilkinson, *The Seven Laws of the Learner* (Sisters, Oregon: Multnomah Books, 1992), 185.

CHAPTER FOUR: PREPARING INTERPRETATION QUESTIONS

1. Lederer, *Anguished English*, 31–35.

2. Hans Finzel, *Observe Interpret Apply* (Wheaton, Ill.: Victor Books, 1994), 46–47.

3. Jim Wilhoit and Leland Ryken, *Effective Bible Teaching* (Grand Rapids, Mich.: Baker Book House, 1988), 134.

4. Gleason Archer, *Encyclopedia of Bible Difficulties* (Grand Rapids, Mich.: Zondervan, 1982).

5. Larry Richards, *Bible Difficulties Solved* (Grand Rapids, Mich.: Revell, 1993).

CHAPTER FIVE: PREPARING APPLICATION QUESTIONS

1. Wilkinson, *The Seven Laws of the Learner*, 146.
2. Charles Spurgeon, *Lectures to My Students* (Lynchburg, Va.: The Old-Time Gospel Hour).
3. W. E. Sangster, *Power in Preaching* (Nashville: Abingdon Press, 1958), 100.

CHAPTER SEVEN: GUIDELINES FOR EFFECTIVE QUESTIONS

1. Petras, *The 776 Stupidest Things Ever Said*, 29, 64, 75–76, 108, 184–86.
2. Joseph Bayly, *I Love Sunday School* (Elgin, Ill.: David C. Cook Publishers, 1987), 25.
3. Kathryn Lindskoog, Creative Writing (Grand Rapids, Mich.: Zondervan, 1989), 244.
4. William Wilen and Ambrose Clegg, Jr., "Effective Questions and Questioning: A Research Review," Theory and Research in Social Education 14, no. 2 (Spring 1986): 154.
5. Joseph Lowman, *Mastering the Techniques of Teaching* (San Francisco: Jossey-Bass Publications, 1984), 135.
6. Walt Russell, "What It Means to Me," *Christianity Today* (26 Oct. 1992): 30.

CHAPTER EIGHT: RESPONDING TO LEARNER PARTICIPATIO

1. Myra and David Sadker, "Questioning Skills," in *Classroom Teaching Skills* (Lexington, Mass.: D. C. Heath and Company, 1986), 171.
2. Richard Peace and Thom Corrigan, *Learning to Care: Developing Community in Small Groups* (Littleton, Col.: Pilgrimage Training Group and NavPress, 1995), 29.
3. Sadker, "Questioning Skills," 172–73.
4. Bruce Wilkinson, *Teaching with Style*, course workbook (Fort Mill, S.C.: Walk Thru the Bible Ministries), 59.

CHAPTER NINE: OVERCOMING DISCUSSION PROBLEMS

1. Walt Russell, "What It Means to Me," *Christianity Today* (26 Oct. 1992): 30–32.
2. Jim Wilhoit and Leland Ryken, *Effective Bible Teaching* (Grand Rapids, Mich.: Baker Book House, 1988), 23.

APPENDIX A: GROWING NEW BIBLE DISCUSSION LEADERS

1. Fred Smith, *You and Your Network* (Waco, Tex.: Word Books).
2. Wilkinson, *The Seven Laws of the Learner*, 198.
3. Smith, *Learning to Lead*, 114–15.

APPENDIX B: LESSON PLANS FOR TRAINING SESSIONS

1. W. E. Sangster, *Power in Preaching* (Nashville: Abingdon Press, 1958), 100.

2. Charles Arn, Win Arn, and Donald McGavran, *Growth: A New Vision for the Sunday School* (Pasadena, Calif.: Church Growth Press, 1980), 95.

3. Wayne Rice, *Hot Illustrations for Youth Talks* (El Cajon, Calif.: Youth Specialties, 1994), 50–51.

4. Joseph Green, as quoted by Myra and David Sadker, "Questioning Skills," 141.

5. Wilkinson, *The Seven Laws of the Learner*, 126.